# Zibo: The Last Great Zen Master of China

# Zibo
## *The Last Great Zen Master of China*

Translation and Commentary by
J. C. Cleary

Foreword by
Thomas Cleary

**AHP Paperbacks**
Berkeley, California

## ASIAN HUMANITIES PRESS/AHP PAPERBACKS

Asian Humanities Press and AHP Paperbacks offer to the specialist and the general reader alike the best in new translations of major works and significant original contributions to enhance our understanding of Asian religions, cultures and thought.

"Asian Humanities Press" and "AHP Paperbacks" are trademarks of Jain Publishing Co. Information address: Jain Publishing Company, P.O. Box 4177, Santa Clara, CA 95054-0177, USA.

ISBN 0-89581-916-3    90 116710

Library of Congress Catalog Card Number 88-83532

Printed in the United States of America

# Contents

# *Foreword*

According to traditional Buddhist historiography, every Buddhist movement goes through three general phases: a genuine phase, in which there is practice and realization; an imitation phase, in which there is practice but no realization; and a remnant phase, characterized by pervasive corruption and ultimate vitiation of the dynamic of the original teaching. Buddhist history of the last two and a half millennia, so far as it is discernible from the traces that remain, amply testifies to the accuracy of this description, as Buddhist teaching cycles have emerged from time to time in response to local needs, subsequently been regularized and emulated by admirers, and eventually taken over by worldly interests and gutted for the dregs of such energy and prestige as remained in the detritus of their external manifestations.

Yet the ultimate Buddhist understanding of time and history as depicted in the Avataṃsaka teaching, the most comprehensive of all Buddhist representations, also makes it clear that there are different scales of time always interpenetrating each other without losing their individual identities. An event on one time scale may therefore be of greater or lesser effective significance than the same event on another time scale, while different events taking place simultaneously may appear to have no perceptible effect on each other in one time scale because the causes and effects of their coincidence manifest on different time scales. Applied to the principle of the three phases of Buddhist movements, this means that genuine, imitation, and derelict phases of Buddhism may occur simultaneously while belonging to different scales of time. Again the concrete traces of Buddhist history bear out the truth of this description, in that different phases of Buddhism commonly appear at the same time on one scale and at different times on another scale; in one time frame, qualitative and quantitative differences may exist in inverse proportions, while in another time frame they may exist in direct proportions.

From this perspective, it is not at all paradoxical to find, for example, some of the greatest Zen masters of Tang dynasty China, in the midst of what is ordinarily perceived as the Golden Age of Chinese Buddhism, lamenting the decline and corruption of Zen; or to find indications of outstanding Zen masters and thriving Zen schools in the Ming and Qing dynasties, when the overt manifestations of Buddhism were generally regarded as the very picture of collapse and decay.

From the standpoint of the linear view of time, history, and evolution generally accepted in Western thought, it may seem to be somewhat difficult to entertain, even experimentally, a multidirectional Buddhistic view of these phenomena, but it is even more difficult to glimpse the overall coherence of the Buddhist enterprise without the appropriate perception. What is more, Buddhist historiography is further complicated by the fact that concealment, disguise, artifice, and indirect teaching were consciously practiced as part of this enterprise, often making it difficult for the investigator to identify the source of effects arising from Buddhistic impulses. As Zen proverb has it, "a good merchant hides his goods and appears to have nothing," and "a skillful craftsman leaves no traces," so the greatest of Buddhist adepts may be the one most deeply hidden rather than the one most in the public eye.

Nevertheless, the reality of the publicly known Buddhist may in fact be most deeply hidden, by dint of the conditioned perceptions of the society in which he or she is at work. While there have always been those who "entered the water without making a ripple, went into the fields without stirring a blade of grass," there have also been those who could not avoid notoriety, their "heads covered with dust and faces streaked with dirt." Superficialists have always envied the fame and endowments of these latter individuals, but in reality the task of the public workers was usually the more difficult for their renown.

Zibo Zhenke was one of those heroic Buddhists who was not afforded the luxury of obscurity, one of those bodhisattvas to whose lot it fell to do his work and make his sacrifice in public. Not until long after the martyrdom that ended his unusually productive life was he relegated by sectarian and academic neglect to the oblivion that, ironically, would have smoothed his path in life, an oblivion unfortunately no longer useful by the time it befell him. But Hanshan Deqing, Zibo's famous colleague and biographer, wrote, "For the time being I record the broad outlines [of Zibo's story], awaiting the time when some future clear-eyed craftsmen of the Zen school who continue the *Transmission of the Lamp* can make use of it." Now that Zibo's words have at last been translated into English, we have the opportunity to see if we can make use of them; if at least they provide us with a new and stimulating glimpse of Buddhism in action, perhaps startling us into a measure of wakefulness, Zibo's works and Hanshan's words will not have been in vain.

Thomas Cleary
Autumn 1988

# *Preface*

This work presents primary materials on the life and teaching of Zibo Zhenke [1543-1604], last of the great Zen masters in Chinese Buddhist history. These materials are drawn from the collected works of Zibo himself, which were assembled shortly after his death by his devoted admirers, and from the biographical essay about Zibo composed by his friend and peer, the Zen master Hanshan Deqing [1546-1623].

Zibo was a famous man in his own time, highly esteemed by those who came into contact with him, active among both the educated elite and the ordinary commoners. Zibo was a tireless worker in the revival of Buddhism in the late 16th century. He crisscrossed China many times, teaching the Zen Path by personal example, giving lessons in Buddhist philosophy and technique, and arranging patronage for Buddhist projects. In a dramatic conclusion to his public career, he was arrested and killed for boldly protesting the policies of the corrupt imperial government.

This study was prompted by curiosity concerning the later history of Chinese Buddhism.

After a close study of many outstanding Buddhist writings from the Song dynasty [10th-13th century], it was clear to me that the customary view among scholars, that Chinese Buddhism peaked in the Tang period [7th-9th century] and thereafter lost its creativity, was a mirage. Not only did Buddhist beliefs remain pervasive among the Chinese people in Song times, but Song period Buddhism displayed enough startling intellectual creativity to make a major impact on Chinese high culture and on Confucian philosophy itself. Even the avowed enemies of Buddhism in Song times confirmed and bemoaned this obvious fact.

Recognizing that Chinese Buddhism was still going strong in the Song period, the question naturally arose: what about later?

Studies in Chinese economic and social history had led me into the 16th and 17th centuries, the late Ming period, which deserves to be called the early modern era in China, as in the West. This was the period when the Chinese economy became extensively commercialized and monetized, when the cash nexus began to take central place in social relations, when feudal bonds dissolved, when vernacular literature emerged. Efforts were launched to popularize classical learning and extend the reach of education beyond the elite. It was a time of intense intellectual ferment, reform movements, new ideas. Iconoclastic thinkers gained notoriety advocating individualism and spontaneity, criticizing the imperial autocracy, even questioning the traditional concept of male supremacy.

And in the midst of it all, as influential as ever, Buddhism: shaping the philosophical discourse of the elite and providing basic tenets of popular religion. Buddhism was at its maximum point of diffusion in Chinese religion and culture: taken for granted in popular beliefs, incorporated into rituals marking the life-cycle, blended with Taoist practices and Confucian philosophy, shading off into the radical individualism of the avant garde.

By late Ming times Buddhism had merged so thoroughly with Chinese elite and popular thought that its distinctive message was becoming blurred and losing its sharp edges. Therefore contemporary representatives of the core teaching like Zibo made it their business to clarify the original intent behind the Buddhist teachings, and to differentiate the true meaning from imitations and derivatives. The great teachers of the late Ming carefully preserved and transmitted the Buddhist classics, the great treasury of teachings to which they were heirs. In their own works they used plain, unequivocal language to direct attention back to the authentic message of the Buddha Dharma.

My aim in this work has been to reveal a milestone in later Chinese Buddhist history by letting Zibo speak for himself, and showing him through the eyes of his contemporaries. The work is a mosaic of translations from original sources. These are the clearest, most reliable guides to what Zibo was saying and doing, primary data in the study of Chinese religious history.

This project owes much to my colleagues in Buddhist studies: Thomas Cleary, the translator of so many major texts in Zen and Huayan Buddhism and Taoism, and Nguyen Tu Cuong, a pioneer in the study of Yogācāra philosophy. I also wish to thank Harvard professors Masayoshi Nagatomi and Tu Wei-ming for sparing some of their valuable time in this effort. Particular thanks are due to Loh Wai-fong, whose deep learning in Chinese culture and expertise in late Ming social and economic history was an invaluable resource.

# Zibo's Life

# Zibo's Life

Zibo was a famous Zen teacher in Ming China in the 16th century. He was a leader of the general revival of Buddhism that took place in the late Ming period, and one of the last of the traditional Zen men in China who played a prominent role in high culture.

The stories that have come down about Zibo's life and work do not constitute a biography in the modern sense. Rather, they are a series of Zen stories, recounting incidents that are significant in the Zen context. They are meant to illustrate the timeless teaching patterns of the Zen school, as well as certain specific features of Zibo's own life and place in Buddhist history.

Modern readers cannot expect to find in these stories a continuous chronology of everyday life, or the focus on personality that we associate with biography. Particular anecdotes are included for their symbolic value as well as literal meaning. Each story is told to let the reader reflect on some facet of the Buddhist Teaching. Zibo is presented not only as a man of a particular time and place, but as an examplar of the Buddhist life of wisdom.

The basic sources for Zibo's lifestory are the stūpa inscription written by his great contemporary and peer, the Zen master Hanshan Deqing, dated 1616[1], and the appendix in the "Separate Record of Zibo"[2] compiled by Zibo's disciples Lu Fu and Yong Dong.

These writers knew Zibo personally, and loved and admired him. Since Hanshan was an enlightened adept who wrote with insight into Zibo's Buddhism, we can follow his account to give us the main framework for the story. In the stories related below, all quotations not otherwise attributed are from Hanshan.

**1**   Hanshan begins:

"The whole world dies and is born in a long night of error
and darkness.  The gate of sentiment is closed tight, the lock of
consciousness is hard to open.  Those who can shatter them
with a blow, those who can throw back their shoulders and
advance alone, cannot easily succeed unless they are bold and
brave and possessed of world-transcending capacities.

"If we observe one after another all the elders who have
transmitted the Lamp [of Enlightenment], we see that they were
all people like this.  Such people have not arisen again for a
long time, but recently we have seen one in Zibo."


**2**   Like most Zen teachers, Zibo was known under various
names at different points in his life.  In his talks he referred to
himself simply as the old monk of whatever temple he was
staying at.  Zibo 'Purple Pine' was a nickname acquired late in
life.  His personal name as a monk was Zhenke 'Truly Capable'.
Like Chinese gentlemen of the time, he had a literary sobriquet
by which he was usually referred to in writing:  his was Daguan
'Consummate Contemplation'.  For the sake of clarity, in this
book he will always be referred to by the name Zibo.


**3**   Zibo's family were originally people from Juqu in Jiangsu
Province, but for generations they had lived in the bustling
town of Wujiang, by the inlet of Lake Taihu.  This was the
economically most advanced region of China, the lower Yangzi
River valley.[3]  Agriculture was commercialized:  most peasants
specialized in cash crops and bought their food.  Trade was
brisk along a network of waterways that linked the many cities
and towns with the countryside and with each other.

The urban centers possessed countless specialized retail and
wholesale shops, warehouses, and workshops.  They were home
to merchants, brokers, craftsmen and wage workers.  They also
contained government headquarters, entertainment districts,

religious establishments, the mansions of the wealthy and the hovels of the poor.

The cities of the Yangzi valley and the Southeast were also cultural centers, with various state and private academies, active patrons of the arts, connoisseurs and critics, and literary associations. There was a thriving trade in printing and selling books written to popular tastes in the vernacular language of the city folk.

New currents were stirring in Chinese culture in the sixteenth century. Vernacular literature was promoted to respectability by leading intellectuals. Philosophy went in new directions, stressing the need to put knowledge into practice, and to meet the changing times with creative adaptation. Leading Ming Confucians began to sound like Buddhists, advocating a return to the inherent knowledge all people possess. Confucian activists went among the people trying to spread knowledge of the Way of the Sages more widely. An avant-garde fringe among the educated elite advocated individualistic ideas of freedom and spontaneity. More people became skeptical of religion; many continued with the customary rituals without real belief. Chinese painting became more abstract, more challenging to the conventional eye. Many people used ledgers in which they recorded their good and bad actions, quantified the merits and demerits, and kept a moral balance-sheet on their lives.

There were many signs of strain. The spread of the money economy made more people more dependent on the hidden forces of the market and its manipulators. Landlords had to struggle to maintain control over their tenants as money relationships replaced personal ties of dependence. In many developed areas, agriculture could not support the growing population, and labor mobility increased as men travelled in search of a livelihood. Along the coast, the government was trying to enforce a ban on Chinese merchants going overseas. The central government tried in vain to increase its share of the revenues taken from the peasants, but the local landowners resisted any increases in taxes. The educated class felt more and more alienated from the Ming dynasty. Factionalism intensified in the imperial bureaucracy. There were purges and attempts to restrict opinion: criticizing the state became more and more dangerous. In the popular novels of the time, the typical villain is the tyrannical official, the typical hero the common man who resists.

This was the world into which Zibo was born in 1544. Zen Buddhism was already a thousand years old in China.

**4**  Hanshan relates an unusual childhood befitting a great teacher like Zibo:

"By the time he was four years old, Zibo still did not talk. At that time there was a strange monk who passed by his family home. The monk rubbed the boy's head and said to Zibo's father: 'When this lad leaves home, he will become a great Buddhist teacher.' As he finished speaking, the monk disappeared. After this happened, Zibo was able to speak. Before this, the footprints of a giant had been seen in the family courtyard, but after this they were seen no more.

"As a youth, Zibo was by nature brave and fierce, hearty and energetic. He was unusually big. Even as a boy, he was not fond of play. . . . As he grew up, his resolve increased day by day: his parents could not hold him back [from his aspiration for transcendence]."

The "Separate Record" adds that as a young man Zibo admired the *you-xia*, who were traditional figures in Chinese stories: indomitable freelance fighters who wandered the land righting wrongs, helping the defenseless, and intervening to see that justice was done.

**5**  Hanshan continues with the story of the naive but earnest young man leaving home to seek the Dharma:

"When he was seventeen, Zibo took up his staff and sword and left home to travel. When he had gone as far as the Lumen

Gate of Suzhou City, there was a severe rainstorm, and he could not proceed any further. He happened to meet a monk named Mingjue from Tiger Hill Temple. As they looked at each other, Mingjue saw how strong Zibo looked and knew that even though he was young, he was no ordinary person. So Mingjue covered Zibo with his umbrella, and they returned together to the temple [nearby].

"They had a late meal [at the temple], happy they had found each other. When Zibo heard the monks' evening recital of the eighty-eight names of Buddha, he was overjoyed. Near dawn he entered Mingjue's room and said: 'The two of us have a great precious jewel—why is there defilement in this?"

"Then Zibo got out the gold pieces he had in his belt and gave them to Mingjue, asking him to hold a vegetarian feast and ordain him. Zibo bowed to Mingjue, honoring him as his teacher. Zibo had sat steadfastly all night until daybreak. He sighed three times and said to himself, 'Look at it and it has no flesh. Eat it and it has no flavor.'"

**6** Even as a young man of seventeen, Zibo could move people with his dedication:

"Around this time Mingjue needed ten thousand pounds of iron to make a great bell. Zibo said, 'I will help.'

"He went [about thirty miles south] to Pinghu, and sat cross-legged outside the gate of one of the great houses. When the owner of the house saw Zibo, he presented him with food, but Zibo would not eat. The owner asked him what he needed. Zibo said, 'Ten thousand pounds of iron to make a great bell. If you have it, I will accept your food.'

"The owner immediately had the iron brought forth. Zibo laughed. After he had eaten, he had the iron transported directly back to Tiger Hill."

**7**   Hanshan narrates some incidents from Zibo's youth as a beginner monk:

"After returning to Tiger Hill, Zibo stayed behind closed doors and read books.  For half a year he did not cross his threshold.

"When he saw that some of the monks drank wine and ate meat, Zibo said, 'If those who leave home are like this, they should be slain.'  After that the monks were very much afraid of him.

"At the age of twenty, Zibo received full formal ordination from a monk who specialized in the scriptures.

"Zibo went to Dongta Temple in Jiaxing.  He saw a monk copying the Huayan Sūtra and knelt to watch him.  After a long while he sighed and said, 'It will be enough if our generation is capable of this.'

"Later on he went to Jingde Temple on Wudang Mountain [in Hubei] and stayed there in seclusion for three years.

"He returned to the Suzhou area [where Tiger Hill was located].  One day he bade farewell to Mingjue and told him, 'I must go travelling to the various regions to call on enlightened teachers and clarify the great matter [of enlightenment].'  So Zibo took his staff and departed."

Zibo was adhering to the time-honored customs of the Zen school:  intensive study of Buddhist classics, and travelling in search of living representatives of the Dharma.  By this point Zibo apparently had recognized the limitations of Mingjue, and the need for further instruction.

**8**   Hanshan tells a story that suggests the young Zibo was still trapped in a dualistic conception of the goal of Buddhism as an escape from the sufferings of birth and death:

Zibo heard a monk reciting a Zen poem that contained the lines:  "Cutting off false thought increases the sickness / Going toward true thusness is also wrong."[4]

Zibo said to the monk, "That's wrong. It should say: 'Only in cutting off false thought is there no sickness / Going toward true thusness is not wrong.'

The monk said, "It's you who are wrong, not the author of the poem."

Hanshan continues:

"Zibo was in great doubt over this. Wherever he went, he would write the two lines on the wall. His doubt was so intense that his head and face became swollen. One day at a vegetarian feast [still fixated on the verse] he was suddenly enlightened. The swelling of his head and face at once dissipated. From then on, he was riding high. He said, 'If I were with Linji or Deshan, I would have awakened at a single slap—no need to ask how or what.'"

[Linji and Deshan, who lived in the ninth century, were two of the greatest teachers in Zen history, noted for their direct methods.]

**9**  After this breakthrough, Zibo went to Mount Lu, a Buddhist center, and plumbed the depths of Yogācāra Buddhist philosophy, which was a cornerstone of the Zen school's methods.

Yogācāra Buddhism[5] gives an analysis of the causal sequences by which the elements of form, sensation, conception, motivation and consciousness are assembled into the subjective worlds that sentient beings experience and act within.

Yogācāra philosophers never said that there is no outer world (as wrongly supposed by those who classify Yogācāra as a kind of Buddhist subjective idealism). Their observation was that ordinary people ordinarily do not perceive the outer world as it is, but perceive instead the *representations* they project upon form due to the conditioning that has shaped their perception and judgment and sense of themselves.

Yogācāra thought in China was summed up in the phrases 'mind only' and 'consciousness only.' This was meant on two levels. For the unenlightened, the world they experience is made up only of the representations their minds and consciousnesses assemble. In reality as experienced by the enlightened, 'all phenomena are Mind only' because all subjective worlds and times and realms of experience, and their bases in physical form, are nothing but things which appear within the all-encompassing unity of the absolute truth level, the Buddha-Mind.

**10** Hanshan gives the story of Zibo's silent accord with an anonymous hidden adept, as if to certify his enlightenment:

"Zibo travelled to Mount Wutai [a Buddhist sacred mountain in North China, legendary abode of Mañjuśrī, the bodhisattva representing transcendent wisdom].

"He came to a cave on a steep cliff where there was an old adept sitting in solitude. Zibo bowed in homage and asked: 'How is it before a single thought is born?' The adept held up one finger. 'How is it after it is born?' The adept extended both hands. Zibo at once comprehended his message. Later on Zibo tried to retrace his footsteps [to the adept's cave], but he could not find the place."

Holding up one finger expresses the unity of being at the absolute truth level. Extending both hands represents the teaching activities of the bodhisattva, who reenters the realm of multiplicity and relative reality to communicate enlightenment.

**11** Hanshan recounts Zibo's meeting with a public figure, Bianrong, who was a well-known Zen teacher in the capital Beijing in the 1570's:

"When Zibo got to the capital, he called on the great elder Bianrong. Bianrong asked him where he had come from. Zibo said, 'From south of the River.' Bianrong asked him why he had come. Zibo said, 'To study the Buddhist scriptures.'

"Bianrong asked, 'Why study the scriptures?' Zibo said, 'To master the meaning of the scriptures and propagate them, and teach on behalf of Buddha.' Bianrong said, 'You must be pure and clean to preach the Dharma.' Zibo said, 'Right now I am not stained by even an atom of dust.'

"Bianrong ordered him to take off his tunic and give it to a monk standing nearby. As Zibo took it off, Bianrong said to him, 'After you have stripped off one layer, there's still another layer.' Zibo laughed and nodded in agreement. After this he stayed on with Bianrong."

**12** "Zibo called on all the great elders of the time, like Dharma Masters Xiaoyan and Xianli. After nine years away, he returned to Tiger Hill to inform Mingjue [of what he had been doing.] Then he went to [the nearby city of] Songjiang and spent one hundred days behind closed doors."

**13** Hanshan includes several incidents to mark Zibo's growing acceptance in cultured high society circles:

Zibo converts the recalcitrant son of a magistrate; Zibo impresses a noted Confucian thinker; Zibo finds great accord with a high minister who is a dedicated Buddhist layman.

**14** Then a story of phony Zen. In Ming times, when Zen styles were influential and fashionable, many men attempted to imitate Zen language or methods without real understanding, giving free rein to their own subjectivity.

A certain gentleman had opened a teaching hall at Shaolin, a site on the holy Mount Song in North China, traditionally the abode of the First Patriarch of Zen, Bodhidharma. Zibo and some of his associates paid him a visit and discovered the man mouthing gibberish, posing as a Zen master. Zibo and his friends were ashamed for the man, and refused to participate in his assembly.

**15** Now in his early thirties, Zibo encountered the man who would be his chief disciple, Daokai.

"When Daokai heard of Zibo's reputation, he went to study with him. Zibo knew that he would be a vessel of the Dharma, so he kept Daokai on as his attendant, entrusting him with all sorts of duties."

The masters of the Zen school regularly took particular care in the selection and training of successors. Chosen pupils of high potential were polished and honed, often over the course of decades, and exposed to a wide variety of situations and tasks, in order to perfect their knowledge of the practical application of the Buddha Dharma.


**16** By this time Zibo had gained a reputation for sanctity, and this helped him in his efforts to arrange patronage for Buddhist projects. Throughout his life, Zibo was concerned to restore and repair temples that had fallen on hard times.

"In the prefectural city, there was a certain Śūraṅgama Temple that had long been abandoned. Powerful landowners [in the neighborhood] had encroached on its grounds to make for themselves gardens and pavilions. Zibo had a verse which he posted there in the ruined temple:

> The bright moon—its single orb cold outside
> the curtains
> Deep in the night, once it shone on people
> meditating

"Zibo wanted to revive the temple, so he charged [the highly placed lay Buddhist] Minister Lu Guangzu to act as the protector of the Dharma [for this project], and put Daokai in charge of making arrangements. Minister Lu's younger brother Mr. Lu Yuntai donated five pillars for the building of the meditation hall.

"When the building was complete, they invited Zibo to inscribe a couplet [to dedicate the new hall]. Zibo wrote:

If you do not discover Mind, sitting in meditation
  just adds to karmic suffering
If you can preserve mindfulness, even reviling the
  Buddhas benefits true cultivation

"Zibo thought that this should be written in blood, so he
pierced his arm with an awl, filled a cup with blood, and wrote
it out."

Hanshan fills in the rest of the story. The new meditation
hall stood, but the resistance of the local landlords who had
taken over the temple's lands blocked Zibo's plan to revive the
temple as a whole. Twenty years later, with a sympathetic
governor in power, the temple was finally rebuilt. Hanshan
concludes that this delayed success was due to the power of
Zibo's vow to restore the temple.


**17** Zibo was very active in the printing and distribution of
Buddhist books. Printing and selling books was a thriving
business in sixteenth century China, so much so that the early
European visitors to China in those days were astounded by
how cheap and plentiful books were there.
  Hanshan links Zibo's efforts to print and distribute Buddhist
writings with his awareness of living at a particular moment in
Chinese Buddhist history, when distorted imitations of Buddhism had sprung up on all sides, and the original message had
to be restated. In Buddhist terminology, the phase when the
genuine teaching has been supplanted by imitations is called
the Semblance Period.

"The Teacher Zibo saw that at the end of the Semblance
Period, the Path of the Dharma was in decline. He made it his
own task to propagate the Dharma and to aid living beings.
He thought about how heavy and numerous the scrolls of the
Canon were: the result was that [copies were expensive and not
very portable, and] there were people in out of the way places

who had never heard the Dharma. He wanted to get the Canon printed in book form, so that it would be easier to circulate: this would enable everyone to read it or to hear it read, and create seeds of enlightenment. Then the wrongs of those who misrepresent Buddhism would be obvious."

Zibo promoted this project through his contacts in the official class, soliciting the help of wealthy gentlemen. He ordered Daokai to coordinate things. In 1589 they began cutting the printing blocks on Mount Wutai in Shanxi. In such a vast project, many people contributed, many things went wrong; there were many delays and shifts in plan. After four years on Wutai, Zibo returned to the south. Ultimately, after Zibo's death, the project came to fruition. Quantities of book-style volumes of the Canon were printed and distributed, when a certain Wu Yongxian, who had studied Zen with Zibo, became governor of Zhejiang and a senior official in the region, and donated his own funds for the purpose. As Hanshan tells the story, Zibo had foretold this: "Indeed, the power of Mr. Wu's faith was as the Teacher had predicted."

**18** The story takes a turn to show us the shifting sands of belief in sixteenth century China:

"When the planning for cutting the printing blocks for the Canon was complete, Zibo returned to the Suzhou area to tell Mingjue, the teacher from whom he had received ordination. By this time, Mingjue had gone back to lay life, and was well known as a doctor.

"When Zibo heard about this, he wanted to deliver Mingjue. At that very moment, as Mingjue was eating his evening meal, his rice bowl suddenly fell to the ground and shattered. Such was the influence of Zibo's spirit!

"So [to carry out his plan to deliver Mingjue] Zibo feigned illness. Lying in a small skiff, he had someone go ask Mingjue to come examine him.

"When Mingjue arrived and saw Zibo, he was startled and fearful. Weeping, Zibo said to him, 'How have you become so deluded? What can we do now?' Mingjue said, 'I will obey your command.' Zibo then ordered him to shave off his hair.

"As Zibo was getting on board the boat to depart, Mingjue [at last genuinely] repented and submitted. He wanted to uphold the proper norms of a disciple and be near Zibo."

**19** Hanshan returns again to show that Zibo was held in the highest honor by the most respectable gentry families of various localities in his home region. Whole lineages turned out to "take refuge" with him, formally accepting his authority as their teacher. Zibo's contacts among the official class and literati elite read like a who's who of the avant garde of late Ming culture.

Hanshan perhaps wished to remind people of Zibo's high standing more than once, because in the end Zibo was anything but respectable: a dissident legally killed by the government.

To help exonerate Zibo, both Hanshan and Lu Fu include an anecdote to show that the Emperor personally held Zibo in high regard:

Once when the Emperor was copying out the Diamond Sūtra, a drop of his sweat fell on the page. The Emperor sent his personal attendant to ask Zibo if the copy had been spoiled. Zibo replied in a verse that delighted the Emperor:

> A drop of royal sweat,
> A bridge for ten thousand generations
> The Inexhaustible Dharma Treasury
> From this gives light

**20** The story of Zibo's filial piety:

Near his hometown, in an admirer's garden, Zibo copied out the Lotus Sūtra to repay his debt to his parents.

In Chinese popular Buddhism the idea was that the karmic

merit gained by virtuous acts like copying a sūtra could be transferred to the benefit of others. Even though they left home and family, monks and nuns could still be filial to their parents and kinfolk by dedicating religious merit to them, to alleviate their karmic burdens.

Zibo described this incident himself:

"Now I rely on Buddha's light as I write out this scripture. Each and every word has inconceivable merit. Hail to the Lotus Sūtra! The King of the Sūtra is our own inherent nature!

"With this merit I repay my father and mother. May their black karma instantly melt away, so that they are born in Buddha's land, see Buddha, hear the Dharma, and witness Reality."[6]


**21** How Hanshan met Zibo:

Zibo sent one of the copies of his Canon in book form to be placed in an iron stūpa built by the famous contemporary Zen teacher Miaofeng [1540-1612]. Like Hanshan, Miaofeng received the patronage of Empress Dowager Li.

Meanwhile Hanshan had informed the Empress Dowager about the book-form Canon being printed on Mount Wutai by Zibo's group. The Empress Dowager was sympathetic, and provided funds for fifteen complete sets to be printed; at her behest, her son the Emperor ordered them distributed to famous temples throughout the realm.

In autumn of 1586 Zibo came to the capital Beijing, looking for Hanshan, but Hanshan was off in Chang'an, further west, expressing his thanks to the Empress Dowager. Zibo travelled east. Hanshan learned of Zibo's itinerary and hastened eastward himself, hoping to cross paths with him. In Hanshan's words:

"Travelling day and night, I arrived in all haste in Jimo [a town in Shandong], but Zibo had already left the monastery and was at a nearby travellers' lodge, about to set out on a long journey the next morning.

"As soon as he saw me that night, he was very happy and laughed. At daybreak I asked him to return to the monastery with me. We stayed together ten days, our minds sealed in mutual accord. The fact that Zibo thought I knew what I was talking about sanctioned my whole life's work."

**22** Further travels of Zibo:

Over the years Zibo covered the length and breadth of China in his travels, visiting the ancient sites in the Buddhist geography of China, stirring up local support to rebuild temples, teaching by example, persisting in his efforts to bring Buddhism to life.

These stories comment symbolically on the situation of late Ming Buddhism, and dramatize Zibo's work and style:

"[Zibo was on foot with several companions] when they encountered a stream in full flood. Everyone decided that it was surely impossible to cross. Zibo took off his robe and waded in ahead, calling to the others. The water was up to his shoulders, but Zibo kept plunging ahead. When he was across, he looked back and said to his disciples, 'At the gate of birth and death, cross directly to succeed!'"

"Zibo returned to the capital area and [organized the effort] to revive the ancient temple Tanzhe. Then he decided to go west to visit Emei [the Buddhist holy mountain in Sichuan]. He passed through Shanxi and Shaanxi and crossed the hanging bridges into Sichuan, to pay homage to the Great Being Samantabhadra [traditionally linked to Mount Emei.]"

"When Zibo came to Lushan, he sought out the ancient foundations of Guizong Temple [established in 340]. All that was left was a single ancient pine. [At one point] it was sold by the temple monks for five pecks of rice. When the woodcutter was about to chop it down, there happened to be a beggar who felt sorry for the tree: he begged enough rice to buy it back. And so the tree survived by the foundations of the temple.

"Zibo was moved when he heard of this. Now the base of the tree had been cut more than halfway through by wood-cutters: it was bound to fall. Zibo filled in earth and stones around it, and made a vow for it to live again, as an omen that the temple itself would be revived. Later, the tree did grow, and in the end, the temple was revived."

"Zibo again travelled north. He came to Stone Sūtra Mountain. [This is where a sixth century prince] had the sūtras carved in stone and placed in caves in a cliff, because he had been concerned that the True Dharma would be engulfed and wiped out by the conflagrations, floods, and windstorms that will end the age.

"When Zibo saw this, he was moved. By this time the [surviving] stūpa and small temple [were on land that] had been encroached upon by the powerful. Zibo vowed to restore them. He opened up one of the stone chambers, and under the seat of a buddha-image, he found a box containing many relics. When he brought them out, the light from the relics lit up the gullies on the cliff face."

The Empress Dowager heard of this wondrous event and sent her personal attendant to bestow upon Zibo a purple robe as a mark of honor. Zibo declined saying, "I am ashamed to say that these poor bones can hardly wear purple. There would be more merit in giving this robe to someone important." Zibo did request that the relics be taken into the palace and displayed for three days there, then be returned and stored in the stone caves. Zibo also requested Hanshan to write a record of the event.

**23** Second meeting of Hanshan and Zibo:

Hanshan heard that Zibo was travelling west again, so he

went to Beijing to meet with him. Hanshan writes:

"We stayed together in a garden in the western capital conversing for forty days and nights, never shutting our eyes. This was truly the happiest event of my whole life."

Zibo and Hanshan made plans together to write a history of the transmission of Buddhism in the Ming period. They agreed to go to Caoqi, the abode of the Sixth Patriarch of Zen in South China, and restore it. Zibo went back to Lushan in central China to wait for Hanshan to join him there. It was the autumn of 1593.

**24** Hanshan arrested:

Hanshan's connections in high places brought him trouble in 1595. The Emperor got into a conflict with his mother, the Empress Dowager, and decided that he did not like the way she and her cronies within the palace had lavished money on Buddhist projects. An order went down to arrest all those involved in the distribution of copies of the Canon funded by the Empress Dowager. Prosecuting officials sought to recover vast sums of money that had already been spent on printing costs.

Hanshan was arrested and put to torture. He was defrocked and sentenced to exile in the far south as a common garrison soldier. Ocean Seal Temple, which the Empress Dowager had built for him in the capital, was ordered destroyed.

**25** Hanshan tells of his final meeting with Zibo:

"When Zibo heard reports of this at Lushan, he chanted the Lotus Sūtra for my sake, hoping that it would aid me in avoiding the death sentence. Then he went to reconnoiter Caoqi [in Guangdong], then returned to Liaocheng [in Shandong]. He was about to go to the capital to help me, when he heard that I had been sent south, so he waited for me [at

Nanjing] on the banks of the Yangzi River.

"In the eleventh month of the same year [1595], we finally met at Lubo Hermitage on the river. Zibo took my hand, sighed, and said, 'You are serving the Great Dharma unto death. The models among the ancients [for this kind of conduct] were Cheng Ying and Gongsun Wujiu [the friends of as assassinated king, who rescued his posthumous son and insured the perpetuation of the royal line.] What kind of man am I? If you do not come back alive, I will not have long to live myself.'

"I repeatedly tried to comfort Zibo. When I was about to depart, Zibo said to me, 'I will die before you. Later affairs I entrust to you.' Then we parted forever."

**26** Zibo's protest:

Zibo's own troubles with the state began in the year 1600, five years after Hanshan had gone into exile. The Emperor ordered the imposition of extra taxes to provide for the rebuilding of three palaces. Eunuch commissioners were sent out to enforce the new levy, called the 'Mines Tax,' which had provoked intense resistance.

The governor of Nankang City in Jiangxi refused to collect the new tax. He was denounced and arrested, and his wife committed suicide. When Zibo heard of this he said, "What a state current affairs have come to! If eunuchs can kill a high official and his wife, what can be done about the worldly path?"

Zibo travelled to the capital to visit the imprisoned governor. To comfort him, Zibo gave him a verse and ordered him to recite it a hundred thousand times. By the time the governor had repeated it eighty thousand times, the Emperor relented and ordered him released. After his return home, whenever he thought of Zibo, the governor would be moved to tears.

Hanshan continues the story: "Since I had not yet [been allowed] to return to my former attire [as a monk], Zibo often lamented: 'The Dharma Gate has no one. If I sit by and watch while the banner of the Dharma is pulled down, then I am not

applying my mind to perpetuate the Three Jewels [enlighten-
ment, the teaching of enlightenment, and the community of
learners] and to make them flourish.  If old Hanshan does not
return from exile, it will be a great wrong and a great defeat for
my appearing in the world [as a Buddhist teacher].  If the
[tradition of writing Zen history embodied in] the *Transmission
of the Lamp* is not continued, it will be a great defeat for my
life of wisdom.  If I can wipe away these three wrongs, I will
never again go to the imperial capital.'"

Hanshan continues:  "At that time I was at Caoqi.  It was
the fall of 1603.  By express mail I informed those of my disciples
who planned to accompany me [in exile] to invite Zibo to come
to Caoqi.  Zibo's answering letter just said, 'Relinquishing this
poor set of bones, I will dwell nowhere.'"

By his resolve to protest government actions, Zibo was
placing himself in great danger.  The Ming state was notorious
for its harsh treatment of critics, even when they held official
rank; for a monk to venture political criticism was extremely
risky.  Zibo's disciples were aware of the danger he faced in the
capital and begged him to desist from his protests.  His longtime
assistant Daokai wrote him in blood pleading with him to go
into hiding.[7]  But Zibo replied:  "When I cut off my hair [to
become a monk], it was already like cutting off my head:  what
other head do I have that can be cut off?"[8]

So Zibo persisted, despite the growing danger:  "Although
he was slandered in more than one memorial to the throne,
Zibo was aloof and unconcerned."[9]

## 27  Zibo's arrest

Finally enemies in the government struck.  As Hanshan tells
it:  "Suddenly the seditious letters came to light.  In the capital
inside and outside the palace there was an uproar.  Those who
were jealous of him took the occasion to denounce Zibo, and in
the end, because of this, he met with disaster."

In terms of Ming dynasty politics, Zibo was guilty of two basic crimes.

By publicly objecting to government actions (like the exile of Hanshan, and the 'Mines Tax' enforcement) Zibo exposed himself to retaliation by men in power, officials who could move for his arrest and condemnation. A monk without special position at court had no standing to criticise the government's actions.

The other unforgivable crime was having connections with the wrong people. He was linked indirectly with the faction of the Empress Dowager Li, who had patronized his friend Hanshan, and given money for printing of copies of the Canon from Zibo's group at Mount Wutai. The Emperor had a falling out with his mother the Empress Dowager over the question of naming the heir apparent. The Emperor wanted to set aside his eldest son, and name his son by his current favorite lady as the new heir apparent. The Empress Dowager objected, and insisted on the original choice of heir.

This strife in the imperial family had repercussions in Buddhist circles as the Emperor struck against his mother's clientele. In 1595 people linked to the project to print and distribute book-style copies of the Canon to major temples were arrested. This is when Hanshan was arrested and beaten, defrocked and sent into exile.

Zibo's arrest came during a great round-up of suspects in the capital in 1603. An unauthorized printed tract had been circulating around the city that denounced the Emperor's favorite lady and her son as dangers to the realm. The Emperor was furious, and ordered his secret police, 'The Embroidered Uniform Guard,' to arrest those who had taken Empress Dowager Li's side in supporting the original heir apparent.

Lu Fu maintained that Zibo was a victim of a faction who did not mind killing a holy man as a way of striking at certain gentlemen linked to him who were their real enemies.[10] Hanshan says that when Zibo learned there were men in the government who wanted him dead, his attitude was, "If the way of the world has gone this far, why live any longer?"[11]

The tutor of the original heir apparent was friends with one of Zibo's disciples. Another disciple of Zibo's was a prominent physician in the capital who had certain enemies in high places because of his links with the tutor.

The physician was arrested and tortured, but admitted nothing. Searching his house, the police found a letter from Zibo in which he spoke of rescuing Hanshan and rebuilding his temple in the capital, a temple since destroyed by the Emperor's order. Zibo's letter said that it was unfilial on the part of the Emperor to go against his mother's compassion.

This was a capital offense. No one could get away with calling the Emperor unfilial. The letter was taken up by a Censor as serious evidence against Zibo, and when memorials denouncing him came before the throne, the Emperor by law could not exonerate him. Zibo was taken into custody peacefully at Tanzhe, the temple near the capital that he had restored.

As Zibo was being taken away under arrest, he spoke a verse for the temple monks:[12]

> Old man Zibo is leaving the mountain
> Relax, you Zen men in the hall
> Above you heads there's the sky
> Opening the correct eye [we see]:
> In any situation, disaster and blessings
> All come from past causes

## 28 Zibo in prison

Zibo was taken to the dreaded 'Eastern Depot,' where the secret police dealt with opponents of the government.

He was confronted with his 'seditious letter' and rebuked by his interrogators: "You are an eminent monk. Why aren't you deep in the mountains practicing religion? Why do you come to the capital to form bonds with gentlemen and meddle in public affairs?" "You are a monk. Your proper place is to be practicing religion in the mountain valleys. What business do

you have coming to the capital?"[13]  Zibo refused to give any
testimony, and only repeated his original protests.

In prison Zibo wrote these verses:[14]

> The sojourner dares to insist that he's totally
>     innocent
> Recognize that the moment of birth equals the moment of
>     death
> See through them, and death and birth are originally
>     one strand
> Wings walk and feet fly
>
> Perhaps Yama [the King of the Underworld] commands
>     the secret police
> Fiery cauldrons, icey mountains—is there anything to
>     them or not?
> Let me ask you what you have understood
> Our petty six-foot-tall bodies are like reeds
>
> A string of pearls—one hundred and eight
> By chance one pearl drops off
> No need to search outside of things
> Adding on birth and death

On the eleventh day of the twelfth month, after being
whipped, Zibo wrote:[34]

> Thirty blows of the bamboo, to repay an old debt
> Whether a criminal name is light or heavy,
>     what can be done?
> Pain becomes the universe—who can recommend it?
> A laugh in reply—there's the Void
> As I sit, I feel the pain gnawing into my flesh
> Being torn limb from limb this year—is there anything
>     to it or not?
> Bamboo can cause pain, I can tell you!
> With my buttocks in ribbons, I try to sit cross-legged

**29** Death in prison

A week after being flogged Zibo died. The death scene was related by Hanshan on the basis of eyewitness accounts:

"After he had washed himself, Zibo told his attendant, 'I'm going. Please thank all the protectors of the Dharma [back home] in Jiangnan for me.' The attendant began to cry. Zibo scolded him saying, 'Twenty years with me, and you still behave like this?' Then Zibo spoke several verses for the man, and when he finished, peacefully passed away sitting upright.

"[A man whom Zibo had met and comforted in the prison] hurried to Zibo's side when he heard he had died. He rubbed Zibo and said, 'The Teacher departed well.' Zibo opened his eyes and with a slight smile said goodbye.

"It was the seventeenth day of the twelfth month of [the year] *gui-mao* [January 1604]. Zibo was sixty years old and had been a monk for over forty years."

**30** Hanshan sums up his story of Zibo:

"Alas! Throughout his life and work, the Teacher encountered equal shares of suspicion and trust, doubt and belief. When they heard of this last bold gesture of his, people high and low all sighed in respect.

"Zibo viewed the material world ['the four elements' earth, water, fire, air] of birth and death as a worn-out shoe. This was brought about by the Dharma. He always taught people using the verse of Viśvabhū Buddha [one of the seven buddhas of antiquity in Zen lore. The verse reads:

> Temporarily borrowing the four elements
>     we make of them a body
> Mind is fundamentally birthless: it is there
>     based on objects]

Hanshan continues: "I once asked Zibo, 'Do you yourself uphold this verse too?' Zibo said, 'After reciting it for over twenty years, I've mastered a line and a half. If I can fully master both lines, I'll have no worries about death and birth.'

"Didn't he prove it!"


## 31 Lu Fu's picture of Zibo[15]

"The Teacher was very large and unusually robust. He was very awe-inspiring, and seemed ever youthful and unsullied. His flesh was like iron. . . .

"When lay disciples entered his room [for private instruction], he stimulated their development in terms of integrity and righteousness, and warned them against greed and violence. . . .

"The Teacher's heart was compassionate, but his external appearance was awesome. Among his followers there were many powerful people and educated gentlemen of means, and he treated them all with equanimity. . . .

"He always said, 'Those who seek the Dharma with worldly sentiments do not enter my room.'"


## 32 Mr. Cao's picture of Zibo

Cao Xuecheng, whom Zibo met in prison, compiled the "Prison Record of the Venerable Zibo."[16] He described Zibo like this:

"He looked like Maitreya. His mind was like a cold pool. His voice was like a sounding bell, his eloquence like a waterfall. Through his tranquil wisdom and mystic light, his fame spread all over the country.

"When he was introduced to men of high status who were haughty, he often broke etiquette to humble them. On the inside he was very compassionate, but on the outside he was stern and disciplined. The world supposed him to be the Venerable Linji come again.

"He made no distinctions among people as to high and low or important and unimportant: he treated them all with an attitude of even sameness. Thus the lowly and the small people took delight in his countenance, and the noble and great viewed his as arrogant. Those who found his gate and entered it invariably took refuge with him."


## 33  Hanshan's eulogy of Zibo

"The Teacher's lifetime of practice would be difficult indeed to match! From the time he first left home, [he meditated all night, so that] his side never touched his mat. For over forty years [as a monk] his nature was steadfast and he boldly advanced. He disciplined his body with utmost strictness. Those who came near him trembled without being cold. He always sat out in the open, not shrinking from wind and frost. As a youth he followed his mother's instructions not to frequent the women's quarters: all his life he never approached women.

"The Teacher held the Diamond Mind. His only intention was to uphold the Great Dharma. Whenever he saw an old temple in ruins, he resolved to revive it. Starting with Śūraṅgama Temple in the beginning, up through Guizong and Yunju and others later, he rebuilt fifteen temples. In addition to having the Canon printed, he searched out, printed, and put into circulation the recorded sayings of the venerated Zen adepts of ancient renown. . . .

"Whenever he taught disciples in his room, he made them study for themselves, in order to develop their own enlightenment, not stopping until the root of doubt was totally removed. . . . The Teacher was energetic and hearty. When he received people, he did not take common sentiment as the Dharma. He sought people out like a blue hawk catching rabbits. Once he saw them, he wanted to take them alive.

"Thus, when someone entered his room but did not reach accord, his heart was ever more compassionate and deeply concerned. He aimed to cut off the root of life directly with a blow of the staff, so those who approached him intimately were rare. The Teacher truly possessed both coolness and warmth.

"By nature he was fond of mountains and rivers. His whole life he travelled with the clouds and flew with the birds, owning a single patched robe and nothing more, with no place to stay.

"He often lamented the decline of the Zen school. He wanted to seek out the stories of all the venerable adepts since the start of our dynasty and make a continuation of the *Transmission of the Lamp*. He did not fulfill this basic vow, but he passed on the intent when he departed.

"Ah! The Teacher was no ordinary man! His perception was direct and swift and sure—it must be traced back to the people of old. For his compassionate vows and the benefits he brought to living beings, for the way he spread and protected the Three Jewels, we can rightly say that he was one of the physical manifestations through which Buddha responds to the world [nirmāṇakāya], that he was a Great Being [mahā-sattva]. . . .

"I think that the Teacher's perception was worthy of being traced back to Linji [d. 867], and that he continued the style of Dahui [d. 1156]. Because he had no lineage of teachers before him, Zibo never dared to promote himself falsely.

"[Confucians say] that the Way of Yao and Shun was transmitted to Confucius and Mencius, that Mencius died [279 B.C.] without handing it on, and that in Song times [11th century] the two Cheng brothers directly succeeded to the lineage. Reasoning like this, then the Teacher Zibo was indeed a true son [of Linji, Dahui and all the earlier enlightened ones], turning the wheel of the Dharma.

"For the time being I record the broad outlines [of Zibo's story], awaiting the time when some future clear-eyed craftsmen of the Zen school who continue the *Transmission of the Lamp* can make use of it. . . ."

**34** Zibo's self-portrait

The last memory-picture comes from Zibo's brush, two verses on "Spreading the Dharma":

> In a dream I see an ocean I cannot measure
> Standing alone on the shore with the sun about to set
> Going back: the road home is already far
> Going forward: with no ground, it's hard to plant my feet
> Ten thousand hesitations
> Hard to advance or retreat
> When I'm in difficulty, who beats the drum?
> Before the drum's sound stops,
> I've already awakened from the dream
> I open my eyes: has there ever been any trouble?

> Awake I see an ocean I cannot measure
> Turning back to look over the western hills:
> The red sun of evening
> Going forward: shocking waves scare people to death
> Going back: I've already lost the road home
> Thousands of hardships are in this moment
> I wonder who can save the suffering?
> To be able to save the suffering
> Truly observe what's good and bad for body and mind
> Disaster and blessing each have a gate
> One Mind unborn: who is the boss?
> In the arena of love and hate
> Determining false and true
> Distinguishing the clues on the road of birth and death
> Washing water with water, trading gold for gold
> Clear in daily action, skilled at interacting
> As ease, not trampling on the seedling crops of other
>     people:
> The old water buffalo, blocking off the Void

**35** Zibo's lineage

Living in a period when many phony 'Zen teachers' made much of their supposed affiliation to lineages reaching back to the famous enlightened ones of old, Zibo never spoke about his lineage. Where did Zibo find his teachers?

> The precious ground, the empty forest—how many fallen leaves?
> Our former teachers' spirit bones are in the flooding waves . . .[17]

## NOTES

1. ZBJ, 313b-317c.

2. ZBBJ, 73b-76d.

3. Fu Yiling, 92-106; Liu Yan, 190-199.

4. The full verse by the 10th century Zen poet Zhang Zhuo reads:

   The light shines quiescent throughout countless worlds
   Ordinary and sage, all sentient beings are in my family
   A moment unborn and the whole thing is revealed
   As soon as the senses stir, it's covered by clouds
   Cutting off false thoughts increases the sickness
   Going toward true thusness is also wrong
   Following worldly causes, there is no obstruction
   Nirvāṇa and saṃsāra are equally illusions

5. See the work of Nguyen Tu Cuong.

6. ZBJ, 488.

7. ZZBJ, 73d-74a.

8. ZBBJ, 74a.

9. ZBBJ, 74a.

10. ZBBJ, 75d.

11. ZBJ, 316c.

12. ZBJ, 320d.

13. ZBBJ, 74a.

14. ZBJ, 321a.

15. ZBBJ, 74b-c.

16. ZBJ, 319b. Mr. Cao was a *jinshi* from Quanzhou City in Fujian Province who held a series of official posts.

17. ZBJ, 491d.

# Zibo's Buddhism

# Zibo's Buddhism

Zen Buddhism was over a thousand years old in China by the time Zibo appeared. As a Zen master, he was heir to the synthesis of Mādhyamika, Yogācāra, and Huayan philosophy that had been the theoretical basis of the Zen school since its early days.[1] As a man of his times, he took part in the effort by many sixteenth century Chinese intellectuals to disseminate culture more widely and to popularize the classical teachings. He directed his audience back to the classic Buddhist sources, and elucidated their intent in plain direct language. In an age when many dabbled in imitation Zen, or styles deriving from it, Zibo became famous as an authentic Zen master in the old style. In terms of Chinese Buddhist history he was most of all a restorer and preserver of the tradition. Here and there in his verses his originality and uniqueness flash out: the sharp silhouette of a man standing alone exposed in the sunset light.

## 1  Skill in Means

Zibo's teaching work was guided by the Buddhist principle of skill in means. According to this principle, each particular expression of the truth must be adapted to the needs and mentalities of the audience. All teachings are provisional expedients, designed for use in particular circumstances. There are no dogmas, no absolute tenets. The truth as such is inconceivable and ineffable and transcends all limited formulations.

The Buddhist teachings are likened to a collection of medicines, to be used as needed. "Since the diseases sentient beings suffer are numberless, so are the medicines that the enlightened ones apply."[2] Zibo said a Buddhist teacher is like a good general who uses tactics flexibly as needed: sometimes he overcomes his adversary with standard tactics, sometimes with surprise tactics; sometimes he wins using both, sometimes he wins without using either.[3] Victory for the Buddhist teacher meant enabling the student to open up his innate capacity for enlightenment.

## 2   Zen and the Scriptures

Zibo often pointed out the basic complementarity between the Buddhism of the sūtras and Zen. In his own teachings he used the sūtras, Buddhist philosophy, and Zen lore. He often advised people first to study certain sets of sūtras and treatises, then use the methods of the Zen school to bring the knowledge in them to life.[4]   Zibo repeated the Zen school's standard formulation:   the scriptures represent Buddha's word; Zen represents Buddha's mind; they support and confirm each other.   If there is anything in the transmission of Buddha's mind, in Zen, that goes against Buddha's word, the scriptures, then it is not real Zen. If Buddha's word is transmitted without a clear understanding of Buddha's mind, if the scriptures are merely repeated without insight into their intent, which is the essence of Zen, this is not true scriptural Buddhism.[5] "When you master the scriptural teachings, the Buddha's words are all your own words.   When you understand the Zen school, the mind of the ancestral teachers is your own mind."[6]

Like Zen men before him, Zibo knew and taught the many sūtras:   the Huayan, the Lotus, the Śūraṅgama, the Sūtra of Complete Enlightenment, the Laṅkāvatāra, the Vimalakīrti Sūtra, and the Perfection of Wisdom Sūtras.[7]   The sūtras picture vast arrays of beings assembled around Buddha to hear his message. Buddha is shown radiating wisdom into countless worlds through diverse expedient means.   By slowly building up giant tableaux of teaching scenes, the sūtras depict the multilevel complexity of the Dharma as a whole. Zibo pointed out that the sūtras use symbols to convey the meaning: one must get the meaning, not stick to the symbols.[8]

## 3  Zen and Buddhist Philosophy

Zibo's writings show that he was deeply versed in Buddhist philosophy.  From its earliest days, the Zen school employed several streams of Buddhist thought, sometimes tacitly, sometimes overtly.  These were the following:

Mādhyamika, (termed in Chinese *xing-zong*, the school of essential nature) which refutes the validity of all concepts, and shows the lack of definite independent identity in all relative phenomena.  This is linked with the contemplation of emptiness, leading to detachment, unbiased objectivity, and unsentimental compassion.

Yogācāra, (in Chinese *xiang-zong*, the school of appearances) which shows how people perceive and experience as they do, and how to transform the basis of this experience to reach nondualistic awareness and nonconceptual wisdom.  This is associated with the contemplation of the relative reality of the many different subjectively perceived worlds of sentient beings, and their patterns of formation and change, leading to knowledge of how to accomplish enlightening actions within the relative world.

Huayan, (in Sanskrit *Avataṃsaka*, the Flower Garland) which shows a panorama of enlightening activities in diverse forms taking place in all worlds of the cosmos at all times at once, reflecting the universal communication of reality.  This is linked to the contemplation of the mean between identitylessness and relative existence, which shows the interpenetration of all particulars with each other and the universal, and enables the enlightened to operate on both sides at once.

Tiantai, (named after the mountain abode of its founder Zhi Yi) a sixth century Chinese systhesis of Buddhist thought and technique.  Tiantai offered classifications of the sūtras, giving a conceptual map to this enormous mass of teaching scenes, symbols and allegories.  Tiantai carefully analyzed the process of meditation from many angles, offering many compellingly logical, comprehensive sets of categories to guide meditators through deepening levels of insight.  Thus, for all its abstract symmetry, Tiantai was always meant as a practical philosophy. From the inception of the Zen school onwards, there were many Zen adepts who knew and used Tiantai categories.

Zibo taught that people need a balanced knowledge of Mādhyamika and Yogācāra philosophies, coupled with Zen studies under the guidance of an expert who knows how to adapt the teachings to specific cases.[9] Like the classic Zen Buddhists, he was at home with the Huayan worldview, and taught in terms of Huayan concepts and metaphors.[10] He often taught meditation in Tiantai Buddhist terms, and used the Tiantai as well as Huayan classifications of the sūtras.[11] Zibo wrote that the only ones who see any incompatibility between Yogācāra, Huayan, and Tiantai philosophies are outsiders attacking Buddhism.[12] He sometimes taught using Tiantai, Huayan and Zen perspectives side by side.[13]

Zibo used the range of sūtras and philosophy that was characteristic of the Zen school. The classic Tang period Zen teachers employed this body of theory and technique implicitly. Their task had been to urge Buddhists already intellectually versed in the sūtras and treatises to move beyond verbal study and emotional allegiance, to real practical application. Zibo seven centuries later was working in a time when Buddhism was being blurred as its message diffused. Consequently, compared to the classic Zen masters, Zibo was very explicit and insistent in referring to the original Zen heritage of Buddhist theory and reiterating and clarifying its basic concepts.

## 4   Zen and Pure Land

By Zibo's time, there was a well-established tradition in China that combined Zen with Pure Land Buddhism.[14]

Pure Land believers focus their faith on Amitābha Buddha, the Buddha of Infinite Life and Infinite Light. Amitābha is said to dwell in his Pure Land paradise in the West. By the power of his original vows, Amitābha guarantees salvation for all people who invoke his name. Pure Land devotional methods were deliberately made simple and open to all sorts of people. The typical Pure Land practice is chanting the name of Amitābha, silently or aloud, alone or in groups. Reciting the buddha-name is a means of focusing mindfulness on Amitābha Buddha. Believers hope to be reborn in the Pure Land, where they will live in bliss in the presence of Amitābha and continue on their path toward enlightenment unobstructed by the sufferings of our world.

Many Pure Land groups carried out their recitation of the buddha-name in an atmosphere of emotional fervor and in-group loyalty. Pure Land biographies feature edifying death scenes: after a lifetime of diligent buddha-name recitation and pious conduct, the dying person sees the Pure Land opening to receive him or her, and can describe to death-bed companions how their beliefs are being verified.

Pure Land practices brought tangible solace and comfort for many people in East Asia. Chanting helps people focus and conserve their energy: it feels better than fretting and fussing and letting worry and anxiety dominate life. Devotional groups could also function as mutual-aid societies. It comes as no surprise that Pure Land groups multiplied in times when secular society fell into crisis. Like Zen, Pure Land was one of the enduring practical forms of Buddhism in China. By Zibo's time, it was perhaps the most commonplace form of Buddhism.

Naturally Pure Land practices were applied in a variety of ways by different people and groups. For many, the emotional and social satisfactions of group-religion were paramount. Routinized, superficial forms of chanting, and the good feelings of being with fellow-believers could easily eclipse the real religious goal: buddha-remembrance, mindfulness of buddha.

Zibo gave the Zen school's reflection on Pure Land practice. Reciting the buddha-name should be a means of remembering Buddha, restoring mindfulness of our inherent enlightened nature. Mechanical recitation, or recitation done with a mind full of miscellaneous thoughts, will not do the trick.[15] Zibo

insisted that only a pure mind makes possible rebirth in the
Pure Land.[16]  From the Zen point of view, a pure mind *is* the
Pure Land.  Zibo's verse on the Pure Land says:[17]

> When the mind is pure, the buddha-land is pure
> When mind is defiled, this land is defiled
> Since purity and defilement are a matter of mind,
> How can you seek truth elsewhere?
> Just observe before mind is born:
> Where are purity and defilement?
> If you penetrate through with this observation,
> Myriad faults are spontaneously dissolved . . .
> Hail to Amitābha Buddha!
> Enlightenment means sentiments unborn
> When sentiments are born, they kill Buddha
> Killing Buddha, you fall into hell . . .
> Let sentiments not be born,
> And Amitābha comes to welcome you . . .
> Break through at the barrier of adverse and favorable
> Only then are you face to face with Amitābha.

Zibo saw Amitābha as an infinite light with countless
manifestations in infinite numbers of worlds.[18]  He urged his
lay followers to encourage their parents to do Pure Land
practice, focusing them with the idea that everything is imper-
manent.[19]

Like Zen teachers in the three centuries before him, Zibo
sometimes employed a teaching-device that utilized and encom-
passed Pure Land practice as Zen exercise.  This was commonly
known as 'the buddha-name-recitation meditation case' *nian-fo
gong-an*.   The technique was this:  While intently reciting
Amitābha's name, invoking and focusing mindfulness on
buddha, the practitioner meditates on the question "Who is
the one reciting the buddha-name?"

From the Zen perspective, the chanting of mantras is a
practice very much akin to the buddha-name-recitation of Pure
Land.  Zibo always made room for these invocation methods,

alongside Zen and scriptural Buddhism, as means to focus and purify mind. In all three approaches, for Zibo the key factor is the state of mind of the person involved: the goal is to illuminate mind.[20] Zibo warned his listeners: "If you recite mantras with a shallow low-grade mind, you will never get the effect."[21]

## 5   The Three Religions Merging into One

In the late Ming period the tendency of "Harmonizing the Three Teachings into One" was in full force. Many people combined the perspectives of Taoism, Confucianism, and Buddhism in their personal religious life. Public teachers appeared actively promoting the synthesis of the three religions. Many people accepted the notion that the three teachings were complementary to each other, and invoked their distinctive values side by side with no sense of contradiction.

Zibo shared in this general trend, though he himself saw the non-Buddhist Chinese traditions through a Buddhist lens. He knew and respected the classics of Taoism and Confucianism, and referred to them freely in his teachings, usually to bring out their parallels to Buddhist ideas.

Zibo said that Buddhism, Confucianism and Taoism all teach detachment from body and mind.[22] Truth itself is not the monopoly of any tradition. "What is Mind? Those who witness it span ancient and modern. Not only Śākyamuni Buddha was this way—so was Confucius."[23]

"But say, when the One Mind is unborn, is it Buddhist, or Taoist, or Confucian? If you are immediately clear and without doubts about this, then in Confucianism you are called a true Confucian, in Taoism you are called a true Taoist, and in Buddhism you are called a true Buddhist. Otherwise, in every case when sages came forth, a great thief was born."[24]

"If you have clearly understood this Mind, then you can be a Confucian, a Buddhist, or a Taoist. If you do not understand this Mind, then if you are a Confucian, you are not a real Confucian; if you are a Taoist, you are not a real Taoist; if you are a Buddhist, you are not a real Buddhist. Work on it!"[25]

"No matter whether Confucian, Taoist, or Buddhist, first awaken to the subtlety of your own mind. . . . Used in transcending the world, the natural subtlety is called the Supreme Vehicle [of Buddhism]. Used in managing the world, it is called the Kingly Way [of Confucianism]. This is real learning, this is real talent."[26]

"Thus the true children of the buddhas and Zen patriarchs come forth by means of their vows. They may be Confucian or Buddhist or follow all kinds of other paths: they benefit beings according to their kind. They are like mercury when it falls to the ground: every bead is round."[27]

The Buddhist concept of skill in means made it natural to take a nonsectarian view and to regard the three traditions as different ways of communicating the same message. According to the view of the three religions common among Chinese Buddhists, their essential meaning is the same (the Great Vehicle Buddhist message of inherent enlightenment), although the terminology varies. Zibo listed a series of equivalent concepts from various Confucian and Buddhist texts:

"When the myriad things are returned to the self [i.e. the true self, our buddha-nature], there are no Buddhist books and non-Buddhist books. . . . It is all one single mind-light. There has never been anything else. . . . In the *Great Learning* [ascribed to Confucius] this mind-light is called 'illuminating virtue' *ming-de*. In the *Doctrine of the Mean* it is called 'Heaven's mandate' *tian-ming*. In the *Analects* it is called by many kinds of names of differing import: 'benevolence' *ren*, 'filial piety' *xiao*, 'social order' *zhi*. . . . In the *Book of Changes* it became the 'great ultimate' *tai-ji* and the eight trigrams. In the *Book of History* it became 'faithfully holding to the mean.' . . . In the *Classic of Music* this mind became the *shao* music and the *huo* music. . . . In the *Lotus Sūtra* it is called 'the reality aspect.' In the *Huayan* it is called 'the four realms of reality.' In the *Śūraṅgama* it is called 'great concentration.' . . . It runs through myriad ages past, and remains forever, so it is called the constant guide."[28]

Accepting the three religions as equal in essence, Zibo evenhandedly criticised people who misapplied them.

"In recent years neither students of Zen nor students of the Confucian Path know from the outset what Mind is. Thus they babble about Zen or bluster about Confucian learning, but the moment they encounter danger and doubt, they lose their courage and their spirits, and are blown down by the wind of objects. They are totally unable to master the nostrils their mommas bore them with. Really, [a man of false learning] is not as good as a guy in a village of three families, however ignorant, who just plants the fields and provides a lot of food for people to eat."[29]

"It is just that fools do not comprehend their own minds. Their emotional views have not been eliminated, and they give rise to false judgments. Within Confucianism, they are tied down by Confucianism; within Taoism, they are killed by Taoism; within Buddhism, they are entangled by Buddhism. [Studying religion like this without practical application to mind] is like putting on fine silk to walk through a forest of thorns."[30]

## 6  Zibo on Taoism

In his early years Zibo became familiar with the Taoist classics, *Lao Zi* and *Zhuang Zi*. As a mature Buddhist teacher he was willing to work within the forms of popular Taoism, which he saw as alternative expressions of real religion.[31] The deities of popular Taoism Zibo readily interpreted as other manifestations of buddhas and bodhisattvas.

Zibo criticized the escapist tendency he saw among some Taoists, and their naive self-interested hopes of preserving physical life. "Sick and tired of the limitations of evanescent life and the impermanence of life and happiness, they admire the way of the immortals, and hope by using it to prolong life and enjoy happiness forever."[32]

Zibo also faulted those Taoists who get absorbed in their

mystic raptures, but neglect to cultivate the seeds of enlightenment.[33]  The Buddhist view is that ecstatic states may be the
by-product of genuine religious practice, but are not its aim.
Those who get attached to ecstatic blissful states cannot function
as enlightening beings, who must be free to come and go in both
pure and impure realms.   Buddhists who cling to emptiness
make a similar mistake, according to Zibo: "It is the same as
when they read *Zhuang Zi*: it makes their souls roam on high
beyond the turbid world. Once they have experienced this sense
of being empty and content, if they think that this is the ultimate,
they will never seek to advance."[34]

## 7  Zibo and Confucianism

Zibo frequently promoted the standard Confucian values
in his teachings.  Zibo accepted Confucius as a true sage, who
showed the flexibility and responsiveness of a sage's skill in
means.[35]  He urged his listeners to emulate Confucius's favorite
disciple Yan Hui for his ability to recognize his faults and not
repeat them.[36]  Zibo often cited classical exemplars of steadfast
purpose and zeal for learning taken from the historical lore
that was basic in Confucianism.  To certain audiences, he
invoked explicitly Confucian virtues: "Within the world let us
always be sprouts of integrity and filial piety."[37]

From a Buddhist standpoint, Zibo advised gentlemen on
how to be good Confucians. He told them they had to find the
mind of Confucius and Mencius within themselves: "When
you find your own inherent mind, you will have found the mind
of Confucius and Mencius."[38]  He chided contemporary Confucians for not knowing where to look for the 'lost mind' that
Mencius said one should seek.[39]

Like many Confucian critics, Zibo pointed out the short-
comings of contemporary 'rote Confucianism' *su-ru*.  He said
that mechanical performance of ritual obligations does not
constitute real filial piety, and in fact adds to bad karma.[40]
Most well-off young men in Ming times received their Confucian

education as an exercise in rote learning, under the pressure of family ambitions for them to succeed in the examinations which brought official rank. Zibo remarked that it was like pouring oil on a fire, to use the ambition-driven examination system to pick officials, officials who ought to be the guardians of the Tao, the moral orientation of society.[41]

Zibo offered an unsparing critique of the contemporary schools of Confucianism that were closest in perspective to Zen Buddhism, the Wang Yangming school and its offshoots. These Confucians emphasized that all people possess an inherent faculty for correct moral judgment, *liang-zhi*, which can be activated through the proper cultivation of mind. They stressed the necessary unity of knowledge and action, and followed a program of Zen-style quiet sitting (to let innate knowledge surface) along with cultural, educational and political work in the world (to test moral knowledge by applying it in real situations). Many sixteenth century Confucians of this stripe worked hard as educators to reawaken people's minds to the inspiration of the classics. They held forth an ideal of spontaneously correct adaptive action very much like the Zen description of a bodhisattva's uncontrived compassion.

Zibo saw most followers of the *liang-zhi* philosophy going wrong by accepting a conditioned, limited range of awareness as the whole of mind, as inherent mind.[42] The effect of this error was to confine people within their own subjectivity, "accepting sentiments as reality-nature."[43] Unwittingly, complacently, they foster their subjectivity by mistaking it for objectivity, and leave their real innate enlightened awareness dormant. "What is worse, they accept the knowing subject as their master, and consider that it sees reality, that it is innate knowledge *liang-zhi*. Alas! This is calling the slave the master. What could be worse?"[44]

## 8   Zibo, Buddhist first

In general Zibo seems to have accepted and used Confucian

and Taoist ideas to the extent that they could be taken as parallel to Buddhist concepts. But once in a while he explicitly stated that Buddhism went beyond the other two. "Though Confucian philosophy has its faults, it is far superior to vulgar learning. Though Zen studies have their faults, they are far superior to Confucian learning."[45] On one occasion he expressed alarm at seeing Buddhist and non-Buddhist books lying jumbled together on a desk, and said that trying to reach enlightenment without Buddhist methods is like steaming sand to make rice.[46] He pointed out that the evidence of Yogācāra philosophy makes it ridiculous to claim, as Chinese detractors of Buddhism did, that there is nothing in Buddhism not already present in the Confucian and Taoist classics.[47]

For all three religions, Zibo held to the criterion of getting results. Those who study must awaken to the light of mind and learn how to use it freely, passing beyond their dependency on the sages, whether Śākyamuni Buddha, Confucius, or Lao Zi.[48] Zibo deplored the kind of shallow eclecticism found among seekers moving impulsively from one tradition to another, without taking the time and effort to master any one of them. "I ask you: Have you actually reached the realm of Confucius and Mencius or not? If you had, you certainly would not act this way. If you have not even mastered Confucianism, how can you study Buddhism? If you have not mastered Buddhism, what spare time is there to study Taoism?"[49]

Thus for Zibo it was not so much 'merging the three religions into one', as merging the other two into Buddhism. Confucian and Taoist ideas figure in his teachings, but more often than not they are presented as analogs of Buddhist concepts, or else as subsets of a more encompassing Buddhist system. From allusions in his writing, it is clear that Zibo was educated in the Chinese classics, including Confucius and Mencius, Lao Zi and Zhuang Zi, and the classics of Poetry and History. He certainly respected Taoism and Confucianism in their authentic embodiments, and was prepared to communicate using their terminology and forms.

Religious attitudes and practices reflecting various blends of the three religions were commonplace in Zibo's world. By the standards of the sixteenth century, Zibo was an old-fashioned 'pure' Buddhist. He always took as his guide the classical Zen Buddhist tradition, and this formed the basis from which he appreciated and used elements of Taoism and Confucianism. Zibo accepted the truism that the gist of the three religions was the same, but his own predeliction and chief concern was Buddhism.

## 9 Zibo on the problems of Ming Buddhism

Zibo made brief observations on the fallacies to be found among contemporary Confucians and Taoists, but he commented at length and in detail on the problems besetting Buddhism in his own day. Given that Zibo employed skill in means, tailoring his teachings to the needs of his listeners, his choices of particular points of emphasis directly and indirectly inform us about the condition of late Ming Buddhism.

Zibo always maintained that the religious and social effectiveness of Buddhism, its qualitative level, was necessarily closely related to the moral quality and sincerity of Buddhist monks and nuns.

"Alas! We are far from the day of the Buddha. Demons and outsiders are seen everywhere shaving their skulls and taking on the appearance of monks and nuns. They falsely pretend to be monks and nuns, but they are really ordinary worldly people. This has reached the point that the standards of the Zen school and the guiding constants of the Path of the Dharma have been almost completely ruined."[50]

"To be a monk or nun without knowing Buddha's mind: how is such a 'monk' or 'nun' any different than a common person? Why shave the head and wear black? It is not the demon kings and outsiders who can destroy Buddhism. The ones who destroy Buddhism are the monks and nuns who are no different from common people."[51]

Zibo traced the opposition and suspicion that often greeted even sincere Buddhists in Ming times to popular aversion to worldly monks and nuns. "These days in our pure and peaceful world, we unexpectedly encounter great slanders, great doubt, great dread. Though the slanderers are a perverse, misguided lot, when we trace back the reason [for their attacks], these are also due to us monks ourselves not being pure and clear in our daily travels on the worldly and world-transcending roads, to us sitting in the pit of the commonplace, without deep mission or far-reaching thoughts."[52]

Zibo went on in detail about the faults of misguided approaches to Buddhism. He rejected those who left home to be monks or nuns without sincere motivation, those who "travel in search of wisdom" merely for self-indulgent purposes, those who flock together aimlessly, those who think that looking like a monk is the same thing as being a monk.[53] He repudiated those imitation-Zen men who learned a few bits of Zen lore in order to pass themselves off as profound people, and rejected the self-proclaimed teachers who imposed their own sentiments and judgments without being clear about the true guidelines of the Dharma.[54]

Zibo criticized monks motivated by the desire to have food and clothing provided ready-made, without having to work, and who avidly sought offerings and patrons. He warned them that if they expected to go on living at ease, consuming the products of the work of others, they were asking for trouble.[55] Zibo rejected monks who curried favor with the rich and powerful in hopes of securing positions at the establishments patronized by them.[56] "In general the dusty laterday disciples do not know the main issue . . . they just compete for the evanescent flowers [of patronage, position, comfort, repute] . . ."[57]

Taking up a problem also described in Ming vernacular novels, Zibo expressed regret that rogues and criminals often assumed the guise of monks and took refuge in Buddhist centers. This led to trouble for legitimate monks, since the authorities could not necessarily distinguish true monks from false.[58]

The root cause of the problem of worldly clergy, in Zibo's view, was the lack of genuine aspiration on the part of students and teachers alike.[59] "Of this it is said, 'If the causal ground is not correct, the result obtained is twisted.' It is like a paper flower that cannot set fruit."[60] Zibo charged many contemporary Buddhists with neglecting their basic heritage of the scriptures and the Zen teachings, to follow worldly motivations:

"When people these days read the enlightenment stories of the ancients, they are like mud men running their hands over an elephant. Since there is no feeling in their hands, how can they know if the elephant is fat or thin? Alas! This type makes desire for reputation and profit and obtaining material support into an incurable disease. They take the [real program of Buddhism, to understand] the great matter of birth and death, and stick it between a horse's legs. Was it not in reference to this that the Śūraṅgama Sūtra says, 'When words of great falsity are created, you fall into uninterrupted hell'?"[61]

## 10 Zibo against phony Zen

Zibo spoke out against many variants of false Zen. For Zibo, false Zen showed up in the contemporary intellectual fashions where the tone and style of Zen were mimicked at random, while the basic teachings of Buddhism were contradicted, misinterpreted or ignored. Many in the later Ming period claimed inspiration from Zen. But more often than not, they adopted views of Zen that were convenient for their own purposes, but had little to do with the original message of Zen. It was a never-ending task for Zibo to respond to this situation.

Zibo pointed out the error of those who concluded that since there is nothing outside of Mind, there is no need for strenuous work to realize enlightenment. Zibo countered that it would not do merely to be able to state the conclusions of Buddhist philosophy, without having really practiced and personally experienced them.[62] The Buddhist life of wisdom requires real insight and empowerment. Simple lip-service is not enough.

Zibo likewise rejected those who pretended to the ultimate unconcern and casual ease of the Zen school, but could not meet the test of comprehending the guiding principles of Zen.[63] Many educated men in late Ming China felt an attraction for Zen styles. They laid claim to Zen values that seemed to them to support indulgence in personal whim, or to justify a life of complacent indolence and subjectivism. Against this background Zibo always had to reiterate the rigorous, practical nature of Zen. In his own conduct he gave a living example of the ascetic dedication, deep learning, and tireless service traditional with Zen men and women.

Working in a time when imitations of Buddhist forms abounded, Zibo always emphasized that the Buddhist teaching is not a matter of appearances. A would-be seeker might have every outward mark of sanctity and religious practice, but still fail in his quest if he did not relinquish his dishonest mind obsessed with reputation and glory.[64] Zibo never accepted outward conformity and verbal expressions of allegiance in themselves as the real substance of religion. He pointed out that the Buddhist teaching cannot be judged from the outside, and that it is not altered to win the approval or avoid the disapproval of superficial onlookers.[65] The criteria used by the Zen school to judge any religious claims were direct experience in accord with the True Dharma, and the resulting practical effectiveness.

Zibo questioned the commonsense of those who doubt the truth of Buddhist teachings without having personally investigated them. He likened this to refusing to take medicine when seriously ill, then cursing the medicine as ineffective when the illness does not abate.[66]

Zibo rejected the phony-Zen idea that since the truth is beyond words, verbal teachings are unnecessary.[67] Zibo's appreciation of the value of verbal teachings was reflected in his efforts to have the Buddhist canon printed in a form that would allow it to circulate more easily, and his work collecting and publishing Zen literature. Zibo directed attention back to these classic sources so that people could clarify their views of basic Buddhist concepts, and be able to distinguish false teachings from true.

Later Ming China witnessed a final wave of the diffusion of Zen ideas into philosophy, art, personal styles of freedom, and ideals of social action. As Zen-derived material was diffused more widely, it lost its sharpness of definition, and was interpreted and applied in diverse ways.

Zen was claimed as an inspiration by many who had only fragmentary ideas of what the Zen school taught: pure subjectivists, libertines, nihilists, antinomians, believers in personal expression and spontaneity, advocates of freedom from social convention. Opponents of these intellectual trends branded them "Crazy Zen" *kuang-chan.*

The word 'Zen' thus became associated with eccentric self-indulgence. Attempts to imitate Zen language produced strange, meaningless phraseology. This is why Zibo put so much emphasis on discipline and sincere motivation. This is why he insisted that real Zen Buddhists must meet the test of the scriptures and the classic Zen lore. In response to those who accepted their own subjectivity as 'inherent mind' and did what they wanted, or what they felt was needed, Zibo constantly cited the objective standards of spiritual attainment put forth in the scriptures and Zen classics.

It seems that Zibo was well aware of the historical moment he faced:

> Karmic consciousness vast and vague
> Not knowing how to stop.
> Ignorance is the water for the boat of dreams
> The wind of unenlightenment roils the mind-sea
> Sails opened amidst the great waves
> Are not easily gathered in[68]

> The home of the ancestral teachers
> Is a stretch of idle ground
> What can be done?

The descendants are too lazy to plough
At length it's sunk back to wilderness
Unless [the descendants] have true bones
Deception rushes on and on[69]


## 11   Zibo on real Zen

Against the tide of phenomena associated with the beginning
of the End of the Dharma in China, Zibo upheld a clear positive
teaching of the Buddhist message.  He interacted with people
up and down the social scale, showing the meaning of the Zen
life by personal example, cutting directly through both the
skepticism of the worldly and the sweet dreams of the pious.

Zibo presented to his audience the classic Buddhist ideal of
the bodhisattva.  The bodhisattva does not view the world
through his or her own sentiments and dislikes.  Since the
bodhisattva does not have the mentality of self versus others,
phenomena do not have to be pushed away.  All things adverse
and favorable become teachers.[70]  The bodhisattva does not
engender false states of mind because she or he does not fall
into the trap of seeing things as existing outside of the buddha-
mind; thus he or she can transform things into the scenery of
the site of enlightenment, and not be transformed by them into
a deluded sentient being tied down by attachments.[71]

Freed from self-other dualism, the bodhisattva is capable
of true compassion.  In Buddhist terms, true compassion is
distinct from the sentimental gestures satisfying self-reflective
interests (the desire to "be good") that are conventionally
thought of as "compassion".  The compassion of bodhisattvas
proceeds from detachment.  Awakening is the prerequisite for
freedom from biases:  compassion comes naturally with awakening.[72]  "All kinds of things, the things that [otherwise] would
become the obstructions of self, are empty without having to be
emptied, are pure without having to be purified."[73]

Just as Buddhist compassion does not mean sentimental
attempts at altruism, Buddhist detachment does not entail being

unfeeling. As Zibo explained: "How could the sages be without feelings? It's just that they penetrate through them and are not beclouded by them. They have feelings, but without entanglements. With feelings, there is nowhere they do not reach. Having no entanglements, there is never any love or hate. This is why the great bodhisattvas transform themselves into mountains of food in famine years, and into various kinds of medicines in times of plague."[74]

For learners, who are would-be bodhisattvas, Zibo stressed that the study of Buddhism must be grounded in the correct teaching.[75] "If you practice without knowing how, then even if you relinquish countless bodies and lives, in the end, it forms karma and suffering."[76] Attempts at "practice" based on arbitrary sentiments will only strengthen the subject-object duality.[77] Zibo was emphatic on this point. "When the perfected people established their teachings, they could hardly all be totally the same, but on the point of reaching the basis [buddhamind] and forgetting sentiments, the thousand paths are one."[78]

Zibo taught his students to use everyday circumstances to further their Buddhist development. "If you are able to use unwished-for situations as your teachers and stepping stones, then wherever you go there are strict teachers and spiritual friends."[79]

On one occasion Zibo gave the disciples travelling with him a lesson in the relativity of satisfactions and desires. He challenged them to compare their own easy lot with the life of hard labor of the boatmen working to propel them.[80]

Zibo often said that suffering itself could be used as a teacher.[81] "Whoever would get out of birth and death must first get to know suffering. If you do not know suffering, you will inevitably think that [the things that bring] suffering are pleasurable. Once you have done this, there is no turning back. Once deluded, forever deluded: when will you get out?"[82]

When a Buddhist layman he knew suffered the loss of loved ones, Zibo advised him to take it as a Buddhist lesson: "If we discuss such things in terms of conventional feelings, they are surely painful and regretable. If we contemplate them with the eye of the Dharma, how do we know that all those who died were not bodhisattvas, demonstrating these scenes of impermanence to make all of you feel fear and realize that this world is not solid?"[83]

Flexible and down-to-earth in the Zen tradition, Zibo taught his students to take every opportunity amidst the ups and downs of life to exercise the Buddhist methods they were learning. This is Buddhist practice-in-the-moment for people seeking an entry into reality.

> How many happy songs, how many sad?
> Finally realizing that outside of Mind
> There is nothing else,
> All situations, adverse and favorable,
> Are our Teachers.[84]

Using the perspectives of Yogācāra Buddhism and the Śūraṅgama Sūtra in the Zen manner, Zibo regularly taught his disciples to contemplate by disassembling their own perceptual experience of self and world into its constituent elements: form, sensation, perception, evaluation and motivation, consciousness; sense-faculties (sight, hearing, taste, smell, touch, conceptual mind), and the associated sense-objects and consciousnesses.

The aim of contemplation along these lines was to refine away sentimental biases and break free of subject-object dualism. Freedom from relativity would bring independence from suffering. When self and other are not placed in opposition, sensory experience is a channel to reality.[85]

"Things and self are forgotten, but the illumination is not lifeless. The luminous source in wondrous clarity sprinkles its waters everywhere on all the parched and withered trees. Moistened with its sweet dew, the dried out trees bloom luxuriantly."[86]

Our own culture's limited view of human possibilities may make it seem to us that Zibo was proposing a daunting task, but in principal his teaching was optimistic and open to all, based on faith that all people have buddha-nature.

"The seeds of enlightenment exist throughout the lands of the dusts. When spring returns to the earth, everything comes to life. In order to become buddha in the future, accompanied by a retinue of associates, and spreading the transformative influence of the Great Dharma, you must plant the seeds today. Ah! The effort is small, but the harvest is great. A real person must take it up!"[87]

Zibo presented learning Buddhism as a process. Eventual enlightenment depends on a balance of developmental influences: it cannot be gained automatically by clever understanding or austerities.[88] Learning Buddhism requires both true aspiration on the part of the student and a clear-eyed enlightened teacher who can apply and adapt the teachings.[89] "The teachings require a teacher for their inner truth to be developed perfectly. When inner truth is perfect, then practice will not be one-sided, and correct results will surely be had in abundance."[90]

The student's own correct effort is indispensable, as Zibo explains: "This key link cannot be given to you by the buddhas or patriarchs, by enlightened teachers or Dharma masters. All they can do is provide encouragement and assistance. . . . It's up to you yourself: you do not depend on anyone else's power. Even though we have the sagely teachings of the Great Canon, these too are no more than words to encourage and assist us."[91]

The student starts by relying on the verbal teachings of the scriptures to investigate the "heart and marrow" of the buddhas. By practicing generosity and repentance, petty states of mind are gradually recast to merge with the Great Mind of enlightenment.[92]

The student's sincerity opens the way to meet true teachers: "With a straightforward mind, tell them the intention you harbor. They will certainly not spurn your true sincerity. They are sure to point out for you methods of finding a living road. Accept their words directly: do not try to figure them out, do not pretend to be intelligent and make up bogus opinions. A newborn baby's thought is only of milk: he does not know whether his mother is pretty or plain, high ranking or lowly."[93]

Zibo says it is up to the learner to work carefully and unstintingly as the teacher directs. Success will come from a hidden direction: "If you do not retreat from your true mind, all the buddhas of the ten directions, and all the celestial powers, will surely feel compassion for you and help you in mysterious ways. Suddenly you penetrate through: the Great Work is completely accomplished."[94]

With this transformation of the basis of experience, one is ready for the bodhisattva career. The bodhisattva is immune to the blandishments of the world, and thus ready to share in dream-like subjective environments to help the beings who make their homes there.[95] The goal is not individual enlightenment, but universal salvation.

"Don't dare be lazy! After you have accepted and upheld the scripture, enlightened knowledge will open up for you. You must not stop with your own individual good. You must vow to be like a lamp that spreads the light to thousands and thousands of lamps, from which the light can be transmitted ad infinitum."[96]

"Having awakened to this truth, you use truth to control sentiments. When sentiments are exhausted, you return to the basis. When you have recovered the basis [buddha-mind], you pity all those who have not yet recovered it. So you ride on the wheels of wisdom and vows to transform everything, crushing and cutting off the root of ignorance. You are only content when, together with all beings, you ascend to supreme enlightenment. This is the attitude of the sages. Thus it is said, 'The pure body of reality [Dharmakāya] fundamentally does not appear or disappear. By the power of the vows of great compassion, it appears to take on birth.'"[97]

"You wander freely on Vairocana's head, propagating the teaching amidst current conditions. You repudiate the dishonesty of the 'heroes' who study Zen in a dead way and strike down with blows and shouts the habit patterns of ignorant fellows. If you are like this, not only do you comprehend [the truth] for yourself, but you also act on behalf of other people. Isn't this very special?"[98]

Zibo saw the life of wisdom not as a remote myth, but as an ever-adaptable living road for ancient and modern, that contemporaries ought to travel.

"There are many kinds of potentials and circumstances with enlightened teachers. Some do the work of the buddhas by means of compassion, some do it by anger. Some do the work of the buddhas by harmonizing with the light while joining with the dusts. Some do the work of the buddhas with scoldings and blows and shouts. Some do the work of the buddhas by respectfully supporting Buddhist endeavors. Some do the work of the buddhas by being disciplined, some by being learned, some by being transcendent and free, some by being stern and strict. Some do the work of the buddhas by making people happy, some by making people afraid. Thus it is said, 'Going against or going along: it's all skill in means.'"[99]

## 12    Zibo in Chinese Buddhist history

Zibo and Hanshan appear as two lofty figures coming near the end of the thousand-year road of Zen Buddhism in China. Without famous predecessors or illustrious descendants, they were among the last Zen masters who were public figures of renown and influence in Chinese high culture. As the seventeenth century wore on, the wisdom of the Zen school was sown in other fields beyond the traditional forms of Buddhism.

Zibo and Hanshan were leaders in the sixteenth century Buddhist revival. They were active in restoring temples, assembling and preserving Buddhist literature, and arranging patronage for Buddhist projects. First and foremost, by their living example and direct presence as teachers they communicated to their time what Zen could be.

The late Ming era was a period of ideological tension and diversity to a degree unusual in Chinese intellectual history.

There was chronic conflict between the central executive and the well-off educated class that supplied officials: calls to end corruption and to return to pure values, accusations of factionalism and disloyalty. New economic relationships spread across the country, and new forms of social conflict arose. Dissident thinkers became famous openly advocating new ideas of self and society. Literature written in the vernacular language and dealing with the concerns of the common man emerged into prominence.

Amidst all this cultural ferment, concepts coming from the Zen tradition were particularly prominent. The new mainstream of Confucianism borrowed substantially from the Zen outlook, as did the more extreme avant-garde. Even those who sought a way out of the dissension of the age by a return to pure Confucian values, who tended to oppose Buddhism for promoting subjectivism, echoed the theme so prominent in the Zen teaching of Zibo and Hanshan: returning to the original inspiration of the classics to bring clarity to a confused situation.

But at this last maximum point of diffusion, this last high tide running farthest up the beach, Zen spread out beyond recognition. The more people took up Zen in a fragmentary, derivative manner, the more its methods and teachings were vitiated by being adopted purely as philosophy, or as styles, or as an aesthetic of personal expression. Zen discourse was often appropriated in a disjointed way and its integral meaning was blurred and lost.

At the same time, shedding their specific Zen form, enlightening elements of the Zen school merged into various contemporary developments beyond Buddhism. Zen was of course intimately involved in the late Ming intellectual movement for popular education by spreading the knowledge of the gist of the classics. Zen currents also fed into the first manifestations of what was to be the new philosophy of the seventeenth and eighteenth century. The Zen critique of the subjectivism of pseudo-Zen and the Wang Yangming school of Confucianism helped prepare the way for the next era's stress on recovering the original meaning of the classics, and the demand for empirical research.

Compared to his illustrious ancestors in the Zen family Zibo was a restorer and preserver, not an innovator or inventor of new forms. By his use of simple straightforward language and his emphasis on the basics of Buddhism, Zibo seems to have deliberately broken with the trend of Zen writings since the thirteenth century to become more and more intricate and self-referential. Unlike the general run of "Zen masters" in the Ming period, Zibo refused to claim for himself an affiliation to an ancient Zen lineage. In direct opposition to his contemporaries for whom Zen could mean whatever they wished it to mean, Zibo constantly related Zen practices and sayings back to their basis in Buddhist scriptures and philosophy.

Zibo embraced the totality of the religious project of Great Vehicle Buddhism, through the synthesis of methods customary in the Zen school. Like his great predecessors, he had the ability to adapt the teachings and carry them into practice in the contemporary situation. In terms of Buddhist learning, he was familiar with the full range of Zen lore and sūtras and śāstras that were traditional in the Zen school. His writings show mastery of these teachings, not blind allegiance or rote repetition. He was flexible and pragmatic, not rigid and dogmatic, able to work within a variety of forms, regarding none as sacrosanct. His teaching words include not only static definitions of concepts, but also dynamic 'turning words' capable of interacting with the mind of the learner and revealing multiple levels of intimate meaning. In all these respects, Zibo met the ancient criteria for the adept teachers of the Zen school.

Zibo came near the end of Zen history, not the beginning. He was aware of where Buddhist history stood in China, and the trends of the times. He was fortified by the knowledge that even when the forms of Buddhism are counterfeited and subside into ineffectiveness and eventually disappear, the Dharma itself always abides.

"The bluegreen mountain is timeless.  The white clouds come and go.  Whether the movement of the teaching is open or blocked, whether human sentiments love or hate it, whether teaching centers flourish or go to ruin, these are all manifestations according to deeds . . ."[100]

> Flowing waters, wind in the pines—
>     it's all Buddha's tongue
> True words transmitted ten thousand ages
>     without a stop
> With the two ears, it has always been hard
>     to hear
> The proper adjustment takes a dead man's skull[101]

Finally, we are left with Zibo's own words as the best indication of the nature and manner of his teaching.  They are respectfully translated here, so that modern readers can become acquainted with another landmark figure in Chinese Buddhist history:  Zibo Zhenke [1544-1604], the red sun of evening.


## NOTES

1. ZBJ, 380b.  See J. C. Cleary, *Zen Dawn.*

2. ZBJ, 332c-d.

3. ZBJ, 378d.

4. ZBJ, 349a.

5. ZBJ, 369d.

6. ZBJ, 348b.

7. ZBJ, 361a-b, 370d, 322d, 328d-329d, 332a-b, 342c, 340d-341a, 351c.

8. ZBJ, 383a-b.

9. ZBJ, 380b.

10. ZBJ, 335a-b.  See T. Cleary, *Entry into the Inconceivable.*

11. ZBJ, 330a-c, 367b, 342a-c, 388a.

12. ZBJ, 352b.

13. ZBJ, 382c-383b.

14. See Yanshou [d. 975], *Zong Jing Lu* (The Source Mirror).

15. See items 38 and 39 in the Translation.

16. ZBJ, 346d.

17. ZBJ, 495c.

18. ZBJ, 350b-c.

19. ZBJ, 364b.

20. ZBJ, 356a-b.

21. ZBJ, 384b.

22. ZBJ, 379a.

23. ZBJ, 495b.

24. ZBJ, 360b-c.

25. ZBJ, 377a.

26. ZBJ, 360b.

27. ZBJ, 361c.

28. ZBJ, 361a-b.

29. ZBJ, 324b.

30. ZBJ, 361b.

31. See item 8 in the Translation.

32. ZBJ, 351b.

33. ZBJ, 351b.

34. ZBJ, 379d.

35. ZBJ, 361b.

36. ZBJ, 363a.

37. ZBJ, 356d.

38. ZBJ, 365a-b.

39. ZBJ, 376d-377a.

40. ZBJ, 359b.

41. ZBJ, 385c.

42. ZBJ, 376d-377a.

43. ZBJ, 324d.

44. ZBJ, 346a.  See item 16 in the Translation.

45. ZBJ, 331a.

46. ZBJ, 338c.

47. ZBJ, 379c.

48. ZBJ, 344d.

49. ZBJ, 347a.

50. ZBJ, 376c.

51. ZBJ, 385d.

52. ZBJ, 356d.

53. ZBJ, 357a-b.

54. ZBJ, 337b.

55. ZBJ, 325a-b.

56. ZBJ, 385c.

57. ZBJ, 359b.

58. ZBJ, 374d.

59. ZBJ, 357a-b.

60. ZBJ, 337b.

61. ZBJ, 359b.

62. ZBJ, 340c.

63. ZBJ, 333c.

64. ZBJ, 359b-c.

65. ZBJ, 386d.

66. ZBJ, 324b.

67. ZBJ, 348b.

68. ZBJ, 486a.

69. ZBJ, 489b.

70. ZBJ, 332c. See item 25 in the Translation.

71. ZBJ, 335b.

72. ZBJ, 328a-c.

73. ZBJ, 328a.

74. ZBJ, 331d.

75. ZBJ, 370c-371b.

76. ZBJ, 327c-d.

77. ZBJ, 327c-d.

78. ZBJ, 327c.

79. ZBJ, 358c-d.

80. ZBJ, 385c-d.

81. ZBJ, 343c.

82. ZBJ, 357d-358a.

83. ZBJ, 364a-b.

84. ZBJ, 371c.

85. ZBJ, 336a, 337c, 325c, 340a, 364c-d, 370a-b, 377c-d.

86. ZBJ, 325d.

87. ZBJ, 372a.

88. ZBJ, 386c-d.

89. ZBJ, 387b-c.

90. ZBJ, 371a.

91. ZBJ, 377d.

92. ZBJ, 359d. See item 35 in the Translation.

93. ZBJ, 380d.

94. ZBJ, 380d.

95. ZBJ, 373c.

96. ZBJ, 371a.

97. ZBJ, 327c.

98. ZBJ, 381a.

99. ZBJ, 389c-d.

100. ZBJ, 497a.

101. ZBJ, 488a.

# Zibo's Teachings

# 1: The Medicine of Emptiness
## (ZBJ, pp. 323b-c)

The world that upholds them, and the worlds of all the living beings of the ten directions, are all rooted in emptiness, and emptiness is rooted in mind. Therefore the sūtra says: "Emptiness is born within great enlightenment like a bubble produced in the ocean. The defiled dusty sensory realms are all things born based on emptiness."[1]

It's just that living beings are stuck fast to their sensory habits, which have accumulated over a long time and solidified: in the end they are not easily broken. Thus the buddhas and bodhisattvas first use the medicine of emptiness to cure them of their strongly held to illness.

Worldly people, not knowing the intent of the buddhas and bodhisattvas, see them frequently talking about emptiness in the scriptures and commentaries, and so conclude that the buddhas take emptiness as the Path. They label Buddhism 'the school of emptiness.' Little do they realize that when the illness of the living beings has been cured, the buddhas' and bodhisattvas' medicine of emptiness has nothing to be applied to. With no application for the medicine of emptiness, they then use the medicine of subtle wonder to cure the illness of emptiness. Living beings are stuck to sensory habits, and the cure depends on the medicine of emptiness. Nevertheless, once the illness of emptiness arises, without the buddhas' and bodhisattvas' medicine of subtle wonder, the damage wrought by the illness of emptiness would not be slight. So how could those who think that Buddhism is the school of emptiness really know the intent of the Buddhas?

Some people take the words of the Sixth Patriarch of Zen[2]— "Originally there is not anything, so where could dust be stirred up"—and make the unwarranted judgment in their minds that "if for me originally there is not anything, what sensory dusts are there that can stain me?" Please investigate this for yourself. Given that "for me originally there is not anything," what is it when people salute me and I feel happy, or when people strike me and I get angry? What things are the joy and anger that appear before me? If you cannot directly break through things like this, then the inner blockage will remain forever. Can you dare assume that the "originally there isn't anything" of the one who makes unwarranted judgements is the same as the "originally there isn't anything" of the Sixth Patriarch?

Buddhas and bodhisattvas expound the teaching like good doctors using medicine, like good generals using their forces. How could there be any unvarying method for using medicine or military force? They just investigate the true situation of the sick person or the adversary. If they find out the true situation the sick person or adversary is in, their application of medicine or military force will (effortlessly follow the inner pattern) like Ding the Cook carving the ox.[3] The worldly ones who think Buddhism is the school of emptiness and steal the Sixth Patriarch's "originally there isn't anything" for their own in effect have their knives broken and leave the ox uncarved.

The buddhas and bodhisattvas realize that for living beings emptiness exists because they are deluded about Mind, that body and mind exists because they are deluded about emptiness, and that the sense objects before them exist because they are deluded about body and mind. Sense objects are the things of the world; body and mind are what belong to sentient beings. Nevertheless, apart from emptiness, the world and sentient beings have no basis. Apart from the Mind of enlightenment, emptiness has no basis. Therefore the buddhas and bodhisattvas teach living beings to begin by understanding emptiness and end by awakening to Mind. When they awaken to Mind, emptiness, the world, and living beings are all unattainable. What is called the mind of great enlightenment is like this: when the floating clouds have completely dispersed, before you raise your eyes the bright moon is already in front of you. The 'floating clouds' represent emptiness and existence; the 'bright moon' represents the eternal light you inherently possess.

Someone came forward and said: "From sense objects one reaches sense organs; from body and mind one reaches emptiness; from emptiness one reaches Mind. Please show me, Teacher, where Mind is right now?" Zhenke laughed and said, "If you have no mind, what is posing this question?" The one who had come forward was at a loss for what to do. Zhenke said: "Using mind to ask about mind, indicating mind without knowing mind: is this your error or mine?" He said, "It's my error." Zhenke said, "If you actually realize your own error, then you will manage not to forget it whether you're walking or sitting or hungry or cold, whether circumstances are favorable or adverse or right or wrong. Then, 'Emptiness is born within great enlightenment like a bubble produced in the ocean. The defiled dusty sensory realms are all things born based on emptiness.' Someday you will know for yourself: not only are living beings, lands, and emptiness all in your mind, but even the mind of great enlightenment is unattainable apart from your mind." The one who had approached bowed his head and withdrew.

## NOTES

1. "Emptiness is born within great enlightenment . . ." Quotation from *Śūraṅgama Sūtra*, T 642. See Luk, *Śūraṅgama*, p. 143.

2. The Sixth Patriarch: According to tradition, the Chan succession passed from Hongren of Huang Mei (602-675) to Huineng (638-713) when the latter was able to express his correct enlightenment in a verse. The other candidate, Shenxiu, had said:

> The body is the bodhi tree
> The mind like a bright mirror's stand
> Constantly carefully wipe them
> Don't let dust gather.

Huineng's verse said:

> Basically bodhi has no tree
> Nor is the bright mirror its stand
> Originally there is not anything
> So where could dust be stirred up?

See Cleary, *Pai-chang*, pp. 12-14, and *Liuzu Fashi Fa Bao Tan Jing*, T 2008.

3. Ding the Cook: an anecdote in *Zhuang Zi*. See Watson, pp. 50-51: Ding avers: "When I first began cutting up oxen, all I could see was the ox itself. After three years I no longer saw the whole ox. And now—now I go at it by the spirit and don't look with my eyes. Perception and understanding have come to a stop and spirit moves where it wants. I go along with the natural makeup, strike in the big hollows, guide the knife through the big openings, and follow things as they are. So I never touch the smallest ligament or tendon, much less a main joint. . . . I've had this knife of mine for nineteen years and I've cut up thousands of oxen with it, and yet the blade is as good as though it had just come from the grindstone. . . ."

# 2: The Light of Mind
### (ZJB, pp. 324b-c)

When the sharp sword comes out of its case, the rays of light flash in the sun. It cuts through iron as if it were clay. Whatever kind of wood is cut and carved by it is sure to become a vessel. This is good use of the sword.

Though the sword is sharp, there's a certain kind of fool who only uses it to cut mud: no vessel is formed of the mud, and the sword blade is progressively ruined. This is bad use of the sword.

This is like the basic subtle wonder inherent in the minds of living beings. They do not use concentration and wisdom to contemplate it, but just indulge in clinging to objects, running after sensory experience without turning back, flowing on through birth and death, illusion and suffering ever deeper, with no escape. How could this be good use of mind?

Those of sharp faculties and superior wisdom use the light of the mind's inherent nature to shine through sense faculties and sense objects to reveal that both lack reality-nature. When the work of concentration and wisdom is achieved, right within sensory affliction they find liberation, right within emotional consciousness they reach the light of wisdom.

If you use the sword like this, you are bound to cut through diamonds and jade. All the vessels formed will be strong, complete, and imperishable, filled with sweet dew to offer libations to all. Whoever is touched by a drop will have his burning vexations become pure and cool. He will find immeasurable hundreds of thousands of samādhis: none comes from outside, because all are inherent in the nature of mind.

Thus it is said "For one who makes good use of mind, the eighty-four thousand afflictions are eighty-four thousand samādhis. For one who makes bad use of mind, the eighty-four thousand samādhis are eighty-four thousand afflictions."[1] Ah! The sword is basically no different: with good use every cut is accomplished; with bad use, day by day the sword goes to ruin.

There is true light and there is false light. The true shines through ten thousand ages without relativity. The false is the light emitted when glued to the six sense objects.

Thus it is said: "Apart from darkness and light, there is no seeing essence. Apart from motion and stillness, there is no hearing substance."[2] Penetration and blockage are left behind; stillness and movement are lost—then smell and taste are like perfume amidst shit, like fire in ice. When joining and detaching are left behind and birth and destruction are wiped out, then enlightenment and discrimination are names without substance.

Yet sense faculties and sense objects necessarily depend on each other to exist and depend on each other not to exist. Thus to produce mind based on objects is called emitting the light glued to falsity. Only when you produce mind not based on objects, so that the solitary light shines with perfection, can it be called the light without relativity. 'Without relativity' means that sentiments of inner and outer have been emptied. 'With relativity' means being sealed within the feelings of inner and outer. When feelings are emptied, reality nature is recovered; when feelings are born, reality nature is lost in delusion. Therefore, for those who can turn things around, things become a means of entry. Thereby feelings become empty without bothering to dispel them.

Old Pang[3] said: "Only when I saw Shitou[4] did I get total fusion of the myriad objects before me." He also said: "In daily activity there's nothing else: Only me harmonizing with myself." This is because this old fellow used complete knowledge as fire to burn to emptiness sense faculties and sense objects. Relativity was abolished and no-relativity was complete. Since it was complete, there was nothing external, so there was not an atom of dust to be a barrier to him.

The Sixth Patriarch heard a passerby reading aloud from the Diamond Sūtra.[5] The moment he heard that one must give rise to one's mind without abiding anywhere, he was liberated from sense faculties and sense objects, and the spiritual light shone round and perfect. This is called "seeing the Path before understanding it." Thus it is said: "Honor what he knew and be lofty and clear. Practice what he knew and the light will be great."[6]

In recent times students of the Path have lost track of the source. There is a lot of confused talk about seeing the Path and understanding the Path. At worst they don't avoid accepting sentiments as reality nature. Therefore, in great sorrow, Changsha[7] said:

> People studying the Path do not recognize reality
> Because they accept the conscious spirit all along.
> This, the root of birth and death for countless ages
> Fools call the original person.

For those all over the country who accept sentiments as reality-nature, this really hits the key spot.

Be a real man, worthy of the name. The Sixth Patriarch was originally a poor fellow selling firewood for a living. Once he heard the Diamond Sūtra, straightaway, he had no doubts. He was truly a special man.

When Jiashan turned back to look, the Boat Monk's life was ended: when the son doubted the father, the father had no choice but to capsize his boat.[8]

You have developed the intention of reciting the Diamond Sūtra. If you are unable to use what the Sixth Patriarch awakened to in order to control the manifestations of your mind in the interplay of love and hate, glory and disgrace, then it will always be hard to use relativistic sentiments to return to reality-nature. Then it will be "the three mires, a single reward for five thousand eons"—this is what you should be worried about. Work hard on it!

## NOTES

1. "Eighty-four thousand afflictions, eighty-four thousand samādhis." See *Vimalakīrtinirdeśa Sūtra*, T 475, section on bodhisattva practice.

2. "No seeing essence, no hearing substance . . ." See Luk, *Śūraṅgama*, pp. 54, 78.

3. Layman Pang: see BCR, pp. 447-48.

4. Shitou Xiqian (700-790), one of the early greats of Chinese Chan. Biography in CDL, j. 14.

5. The Sixth Patriarch and the Diamond Sūtra: According to the story in the Platform Scripture, Huineng was working as a firewood when he happened to hear someone reciting the Diamond Sūtra, and received great awakening. This inspired him to seek out the Fifth Patriarch at Huang Mei.

6. "Honor what he knew . . ." Apparently based on a saying of Zeng Zi, grandson of Confucius.

7. Changsha Jingcen (n.d., late Tang), 'Tiger Cen' a great Chan teacher, disciple of Nanquan. For biography see CDL, j. 10 and BCR, pp. 441-42.

8. Jiashan and the Boat Monk: The Boat Monk had studied under Shitou's successor Yaoshan along with Daowu (768-835) and Yunyan (781-841) (see BCR, pp. 456-57). Afterwords he sailed a little boat at Huating (in Fujian). Once he told Daowu, "Later on if you have any promising monks, direct one to come here."

In his wanderings, Daowu happened to encounter Jiashan as he was preaching on the Dharmakāya. Daowu smiled at Jiashan's "explanations," and Jiashan politely asked him to point out his error. Daowu said: "You have appeared in the world without a teacher." Jiashan said: "Please explain thoroughly where it was wrong." Daowu said, "I could never explain, but I have a comrade who receives people on a boat at Huating. Please go there and see him: you're sure to benefit." Jiashan dimissed his congregation and went to see the Boat Monk.

As soon as the Boat Monk saw him he asked: "What temple do you reside at, O man of great virtue?" Jiashan said: "I don't stay at a temple—staying is not like it." The Boatman said: "You say 'not like it'—not like what?" Jiashan said: "It's not the phenomena before our eyes." The Boatman said: "Where did you learn that?" Jiashan said: "It's not something ears or eyes reach to." The Boatman said: "One appropriate phrase is a peg to tether a donkey for ten thousand eons." He also asked: "Sending down the line a thousand feet, the intent is deep in the pond—three inches from the hook, why don't you speak?" As Jiashan was trying to say something, the Boatman knocked him into the water with his pole. As soon as Jiashan climbed out of the water into the boat, the Boatman said: "Speak! Speak!" Again Jiashan tried to open his mouth, and again the Boatman hit him—at this Jiashan was greatly enlightened. Then he bowed three times. The Boatman said: "I'll let you play with the line on the fishing pole: if you don't go against the pure waves, the meaning is spontaneously clear." Then Jiashan asked: "What is the teacher's idea about casting hook and line?" The Boatman said: "The line hangs down, floating on the green water, defining the meaning of being and nothingness." Jiashan said: "The words bring along the mystery, but there is no road. The tongue speaks but doesn't speak." The Boatman said: "When you have totally scooped out the river's waves, you finally meet the golden fish." Jiashan covered his ears. The Boatman said: "Right! Right!" Then he instructed him: "From now on you must hide your body where there are no traces. I was with Yaoshan for thirty years, and only understood this. Now that you have attained, hereafter, do not stay in towns or villages—just go deep into the mountains, and by the side of your hoe receive one or a half to continue our School. Don't let it be cut off."

Jiashan accepted his instructions, bowed, bade farewell, and climbed up onto the bank to depart, looking back again and again. So the Boatman called out, "Hey Reverend!" When Jiashan looked back, the Boatman held his oar upright and said, "If you think there's something else . . ." His words ended, he capsized the boat and sank into the misty waves.

# 3: Worldly Truth
## (ZBJ, pp. 324d-325c)

The Han Grand Tutor Shu Guang[1] submitted a memorial begging to be allowed to retire. The emperor rewarded him with twenty catties of gold, and the crown prince bestowed fifty catties on him. When Shu Guang returned to his home town, every day he had his family provide and lay out a feast, to which he invited his clansmen and old friends and associates to share in the enjoyment. After more than a year, the gold was almost used up. Shu Guang's sons and grandsons urged him to set up an estate for them. Shu Guang said, "How could I be so perverse as to be unmindful of my sons and grandsons? Seeing that they still have for themselves our old fields and buildings, I make my sons and grandsons work hard in them, so that they will have enough to provide for their clothing and food. If I were to add more than now, making a surplus, I would just be teaching my descendants laziness. Moreover, if a worthy person has much wealth, his will is reduced. If a fool has much wealth, his faults are increased. What's more, the rich are resented by everyone. I don't want to change my sons and grandsons: I don't want to increase their faults or engender resentment towards them." Upon hearing this, his clansmen gladly submitted.

Again: Pang Degong[2] was plowing on a hill, with his wife and children ahead of him weeding. The military governor of Jingzhou, Liu Biao, pointed to this and asked, "Sir, you live the painful rustic life, and you will not consent to accept an official salary. What will you bequeath to your descendants in later generations?" Degong said: "Worldly people all bequeath danger to their descendants: I bequeath security. Though the bequests are not the same, it is not that I have nothing to bequeath." Liu Biao sighed and departed.

Both old men were worthy paragons of the worldly truth. Their views were this lofty and enlightened.

If we leavers of home do not beg for food to keep ourselves

alive, but instead covet people's offerings and support, we are wrongly receiving what's improper. When we investigate where this fault comes from, it's just from wanting to wear ready-made clothes and eat ready-made food.

To dislike hard work and like leisure is a commonplace sentiment. But clothing does not come down from the sky; food does not bubble up from the earth. All food and clothing must be produced by hard work. If other people do the work, while I consume the product at ease, and I expect to go on consuming it for a long time, to do so without trouble is impossible.

Old man Shu Guang was an old servitor of the Han court. When he was presented with gold, he did not dare enjoy it by himself, but shared it with his clansmen. His sons and grandsons did not get to possess it.

Since we have placed ourselves outside the four classes of the people, and we beg for food to sustain our last breaths, who besides the four classes of the people will donate things to us? Though the offerings of gentlemen, peasants, artisans, and merchants are not the same, every inch of thread, every grain of rice, all comes from hard work. Having worked hard to get these things, they are happy to be generous to us because they seek to repent their sins and to add to their benefits. If we have the name of monks but lack the reality of monks, we will surely be unable to benefit self and others. In other lifetimes we are sure to switch heads and change faces and become animals. We must pay back their benevolent donations!

If old Yama[3] accepts your slippery tricks and your feeble games, if you can get by with deceiving him, then all the talk of heaven and hell, of the five blessings and the six evils[4] is lies. How could the Tathāgata and the sages by lying to living beings with false words?

Food and drink and sex are the great desires of humanity. If you can actually establish a firm footing regarding these three, then what need is there to avoid cities and towns and dwell in mountain forests? This applies to the highest type of monks, because for them enlightened knowledge is already developed and vows of enlightened compassion are already operating. Those who contribute to the support of this kind of monk will surely be able to wipe away their evil deeds and increase their benefits.

If their enlightened knowledge has not yet greatly developed, and their vows of enlightened compassion are not yet operating on a large scale, but they are able to recite the Buddha's words, and understand a bit of their meaning, then practice according to their understanding—this type is called the middle grade of monks.

If they just recite the Buddha's words but cannot understand the meaning, I fear they will bring the Dharma into disrepute, as they struggle to maintain discipline. This type is called the lower grade of monks.

Though these three kinds of monks are not the same in depth, none of the three come under the category of those who have the name but not the substance of monks. If people respect and support them, their wrongdoings will dissolve and their good fortune will increase, without a doubt. Outside of these three kinds, all the rest are just ordinary people with shaven heads: they are not monks.

Though you have been ordained long since, have you reflected back on the true substance of being a monk with shame or not? When a monk really has shame, should scorn come from without, what's genuine in it, he accepts.

To teach you I have cited Shu Guang of Western Han and Pang Degong of Eastern Han, along with an explanation of three kinds of monks. You should hollow out your mind and forget your physical form. Weep and wail as you read this twenty or thirty times: then in the future you will make a good monk. Start today!

### NOTES

1. Shu Guang was a man of Lan Ling made Grand Tutor in the time of Emperor Xuan of Han. ZW, p. 9584.

2. Pang Degong was a man of Xiang Yang who dwelled in seclusion

with his wife and family, growing his own food, during the Jian An years (196-220) at the end of the Han dynasty. He refused invitations from powerful men like Liu Biao, Zhuge Liang, and Sima De. ZW, p. 4832.

3. Yama, the king of the underworld and judge of the dead. See Mochizuki, pp. 4899-4900.

4. The "Great Law" (*Hong Fan*) section of the Classic of History, (*Shang Shu*) speaks of the five blessings of long life, wealth, health, many descendants, and noble rank; and six evils of bad fortune, shortened lifespan, jealousy, the worries of poverty, evil, and weakness. ZW, pp. 678, 1454.

# 4:   Knowing and Awakening
## (ZBJ, pp. 330d-331a)

Reality-nature is like water; feelings are like ice. Ice is a solid obstruction; water is fluid and flows through. Free-flowing, it is fundamentally without subject and object. As a solid obstruction, sense faculties and sense objects are in opposition.

There is knowing these meanings, and there is awakening to these meanings. With knowing, the ideas are understood, but in contact with things and events, there is still delusion. With awakening, in contact with things and events you understand their inner truth, that sentiments and sense objects are of themselves empty. Delusion is the entanglement of feelings. Awakening is meshing with reality-nature. Entanglement means duality; meshing means oneness. Duality implies relativity; oneness implies birthlessness. Birthlessness is the constant principle of reality-nature; relativity is the transformation of reality-nature. Constancy is selfless and luminous. Transformation means having sentiments and being dimmed.

Thus knowledge within darkness cannot vanquish the darkness, so then the path is no match for habitual actions. With luminosity, habitual actions do not get the better of awareness, so that without depending on cultivation, one directly

enters enlightenment. Otherwise, even if you relinquish countless bodies and lives, it just adds to the karma of contrived
activity. This is because awakening is close to immediate
awareness, while knowing is close to comparative awareness.[1]
Thus what can be achieved by knowing and awakening differs.

### NOTES

1. Immediate awareness and comparative awareness: According
to Mochzuki, pp. 1696-97, these concepts derive from the *Sandhinir-
mocana Sūtra*, T 675, and the *Yogācārabhūmiśāstra*, T 1579. ZJL,
j. 53 gives a full treatment of these categories. Immediate awareness
directly apprehends the inherent essence, "what words cannot reach,
what provisional knowledge cannot link up with." Only immediate
awareness reaches reality, knowing that inherent nature is apart
from words and concepts and intellectual discrimination. (ZBJ, p. 864.)
Comparative awareness is based on discrimination and clinging to
the forms of things: it works by comparing, judging, and categorizing.
(ZJL, 805.)

## 5: Comfortably on Fire
### (ZBJ, p. 336c)

Even an utter fool would fear being burned or scalded if
we sent him into boiling water or fire. Even under com-
pulsion he would not agree to go into boiling water or fire.

The boiling water and fire of the five desires[1] burn and scald
the life of wisdom of the body of reality[2] of living beings, yet
people willingly walk into them, and not for a morning or an
evening only. To the end they never fear them. Have they
lost their minds or gone mad? Overall they judge the stinking
bag of skin to be a vessel of purity and judge the mind of ignorance to be the root of life. It's because they cannot contemplate
the body in terms of the four elements[3] or the mind in terms
of the four clusters.[4] Modern people cannot sleep if the pillow
is the least bit uncomfortable: when they lie down in bed they
are sure to make it comfortable before it will do. Birth and

death is indeed important to people, yet they all ostensibly rest content and unconcerned and don't plan for it in the least. Why?

## NOTES

1. The five desires: can be construed as desires for the five sense objects—sights, sounds, smells, tastes, touch; or as desire for wealth, sexual pleasure, food and drink, fame, and sleep. SY, p. 388.

2. The body of reality: Buddha as Dharmakāya, the absolute reality that all beings share in. "The oneness of the realm of reality is the everywhere equal Dharmakāya of the Tathāgatas." ZJL, j. 36. Dharmakāya can be seen under two aspects as suchness and as the wisdom of suchness. (". . . the life of wisdom of the body of reality . . .") See *Suvarṇaprabhāsa Sūtra*, T 664, p. 363a.

3. The four elements are earth, water, fire, and air. Together they make up the first of the skandhas, or clusters.

4. The four clusters: the skandhas other than the first skandha, form. Namely, sensation or reception, perception or conception, motivational synthesis or coordination (including the patterning activities of emotion and judgment), and consciousness. The body-mind is composed of the five skandhas, according to the Buddhist analysis.

# 6: Truth Is Indescribable
### (ZBJ, p. 338a)

The Dharma is indescribable: if it could be described, the Dharma too would be a description. The sages know that the Dharma is indescribable and that all kinds of descriptions, metaphors, and comparisons for it are no more than temporary expedients.

(All comparisons have their limitations:) If it is compared to emptiness, though emptiness is boundless, it cannot bring forth all things. If it is compared to the earth, though the earth can bring forth things, it has boundaries. If it is compared to water, though water can flow through things, it can dry up. If it is compared to the wind, though the wind can move the myriad things, it can die down. If it is compared to fire, though fire light can banish the darkness, it cannot be touched. If it is compared to a tree, though a tree can produce all kinds of flowers and fruits, detached from the ground it has no place to put its roots. If it is compared to a lotus, though the lotus has flowers and fruits at the same time, apart from water it cannot exist. If it is compared to the campa flower, though the campa is fragrant, when the autumn wind comes, the fragrance disappears. If it is compared to jewels, though they are the most singular gems in the world, they do no equal the clear emptiness and pervading luminescence of the Dharma. The Dharma has been likened to a dragon, to a lion, to a great man, to a king, to a father, to a mother. It has been described as great, as small, as long, as broad, as square, as round, as curved, as straight. It has been compared to motion, to stillness, to curling up, to extending out, to the relative, to the absolute.

In essence, despite the hundreds and thousands of metaphors, the Dharma is indescribable. Therefore I say that descriptions, metaphors, and comparisons are nothing but the temporary expedient methods of the sages as they have responded to beings. For this reason those who cling to the metaphors are stumped by the Dharma: they do not know the Dharma.

# 7: How to Reach the Pure Land[1]
### (ZBJ, pp. 338d-339a)

The sense of reciting the buddha-name to seek birth in the Pure Land lies in upholding the recitation throughout your whole life. Then when you face the end of your life, your mind is wholly unperturbed. You must know that this world is the scene of extreme suffering and that the Pure Land is the site of perfect bliss. It will be like birds or fish whose bodies are in cages but whose minds fly beyond the cage. For those who recite the buddha-name, the world is a cage; the Pure Land is the open water or the sky. Aversion and envy are completely purified, so when the time comes to relinquish life, there is no room at all in their minds for worldly desires. Therefore, no matter how heavy or light their wrong deeds may be, they go straight to the Pure Land, without a doubt. But even if they have recited the buddha-name for a long time throughout their lives, when it comes time to relinquish life, if the habit of worldly desires has not been forgotten, and the contemplation of the Pure Land is not unmixed—though such people think that by reciting the buddha-name they can bring along their karma to go be born in the Pure Land—if we judge truly, for them to be born in the Pure Land is surely difficult.

Thus on Mt. Lu, Hui Yuan first devised the *Treatise on the Nature of Phenomena*, and then started the White Lotus Society.[2] This was not without reason, because if the nature of phenomena is not clearly understood, the barrier of sentiments will not be broken. If the barrier of sentiments is not broken, the clinging perception of body and mind can never be dissolved. Since clinging perceptions are not dissolved, the root of the desires for food, drink and sex definitely cannot be pulled out. Therefore, though the mouth recite the buddha-name, the spirit is running after objects of desire.

First we teach them methods for smashing body and mind. When through gradual practice they are familiarized with these, then they are able to comprehend that neither body nor mind are our possessions. If this understanding is achieved, then even if the clinging perception of body and mind is not yet abruptly smashed, still, compared to ordinary people, they are far more elevated and enlightened.

Of the methods for smashing body and mind, none equals the first half of Viśvābhu Buddha's verse transmitting mind:[3] it is the quickest and most concise.

> Temporarily borrowing the four elements
> We take them as the body
> Mind is fundamentally without birth
> It is there based on objects

Let seekers recite it ten million or five million or three million times: gradually, by reciting the verse, you will come to understand it. Then naturally unwarranted assumptions (of the reality of) body and mind will be greatly lessened.

Once such assumptions have been lessened, take the mind that has recited this verse to recite the name of Amida Buddha and concentrate your thoughts on the West (Amida's realm). When it is time to relinquish your life, thoughts of worldly desires will be emptied without having to apply effort. Why? Because you have concentrated your thoughts taking advantage of your understanding (that body and mind are not possessions).

An ancient worthy said: "First comprehend that body and mind are not possessions. When this knowledge develops, concentrate your mind on reciting the buddha-name and seek birth in the Pure Land." If people recite the buddha-name like this, I guarantee that not one of them will fail to be born in the Pure Land. This was also Hui Yuan's idea on Mt. Lu when he first devised the *Treatise on the Nature of Phenomena* in order to open up living beings' understanding, and then established the White Lotus Society to let them accomplish their practice.

## NOTES

1. The Pure Land: is the paradisical abode in the West of Amida: Amitābha/Amitāyus, the Buddha of Infinite Light and of Infinite Life; the destination of those invoking the name of Amida.

2. In this piece Zibo mistakenly attributes to Huiyuan of Mt. Lu (344-416), traditionally the founder of the White Lotus Society for lay Pure Land Buddhists, authorship of the *Fa Xing Lun*, written later by a learned monk also called Huiyuan. See Mochizuki, pp. 263-64.

3. Viśvābhu is one of the so-called Seven Ancient Buddhas, predecessors to Śākyamuni and the Chan patriarchs, whose transmission verses lead off the *Transmission of the Lamp*. See CDL, j. 1.

## 8: Encounters with Guanyin
### (ZBJ, pp. 339a-d)

I have heard that the bodhisattva Guanyin at first based herself on the ancient buddha Guanyin to generate her aspiration: "If I am to become a buddha equal to the Tathāgata Guanyin, I will myself enter enlightenment, and teach others to enter, by means of the three wisdoms, of hearing, contemplation, and cultivation. From hearing to contemplation, from contemplation to accurate mastery, from mastery to leaving hearing behind: when hearing is left behind, objects are forgotten, and when objects are forgotten, hearing is exhausted. Using this samādhi, influencing them by means of compassion and wisdom, I will overcome the defiled habits of past ages, and remake the black karma of living beings, so that all living beings will equal us enlightened ones. If this vow is not accomplished, I swear not to become a buddha."

So among the six senses, the bodhisattva Guanyin only uses hearing to open up the gate of perfect penetration: her fundamental vow is to respond to the potentials of the beings of this world. That is, she makes sound and hearing the essence of her teaching. Therefore it is not that all the countless great bodhisattvas of the other regions have bad qualities that makes Śākyamuni send them back and only choose Guanyin to come forward: it's that all the other great bodhisattvas are suitable for other regions, while Guanyin alone is suitable for this region.[1] From this point of view, in the path of influence and response, if there is the slightest deviation in fit, then it is not exactly right. Even with spiritual powers and skillful wisdom, even when the fit is exactly right, it is impossible to contrive skillful means. If skillful means could be contrived, would all great bodhisattvas lack the spiritual powers and skillful wisdom to do so?

When I was young it seemed to me that I had a great affinity for Guanyin, but it was not so. At first I didn't know who the bodhisattva of great compassion was. When I was about to become a monk, I suddenly changed my mind. I thought to myself: "I can still practice without cutting off my hair—why should I cut it? Do I have to have a bald head before I can practice?" All those who had been encouraging me toward Buddhism were shocked and very unhappy when they heard me talk like this.

Around that time, as I chanced to be asleep, in my sleep I saw an old monk standing in the sky to the southeast, pointing far off to the southwest without saying a word. I turned my head to where he was pointing and saw in the southwest a boat filled with monks and lay people chanting together with different voices the same sound: "Hail to Amida Buddha!" As the sound "Buddha" entered my ears, my insides felt pure and cool and I was filled with an indescribable contentment. I ran quickly, wishing to board the boat, but I hadn't reached it when I awoke from the dream.

I spoke to those who had been encouraging me, telling them of the strange sights in the dream. They all said: "You aspired to cut off your hair (to become a monk), but then changed your mind in midcourse. You have a great affinity with the bodhisattva Guanyin, so the bodhisattva has appeared in a monk's body to expound the Dharma for you." I said: "He said nothing at all, but just pointed with his hand. When did he ever expound the Dharma?" Someone in the group said: "The bodhisattva used the pointing as a tongue and expounded the Dharma completely. It's just that you didn't understand." When I heard this, my intention to cut off my hair was finally decided beyond a doubt.

Even after I had cut off my hair, due to the habitual defilements of many births, coupled with my fierce nature, even though I had become a monk, I was generally negligent towards the guidelines laid down by the Tathāgata. I did not understand this in my own mind, but it was something that the enlightened eye of the mind of the bodhisattva of inescapable great compassion (Guanyin) was aware of. Ah!

I had been a monk for over thirty years when on the second day of the third month of the *wu-xu* year of Wanli (1598) my boat was moored on the bank of the Xiang River.[2] There happened to be two or three boats alongside which were bringing in loads of incense to Wudang. All night long through till dawn they were burning incense and reciting sūtras seemingly without stop. All of them were calling out with different voices the same sound: "Hail to Amida Buddha!" As the sound entered my sleeping ears, I felt a pang in my heart: this was the scene I had dreamed of thirty years earlier when I was about to cut off my hair!

Now the bodhisattva Guanyin is Amida Buddha's assistant. That group (of devotees) were looking to the (Taoist deity) Xuanwu and calling him Amida Buddha: Xuanwu is one of Guanyin's transformation bodies responding to the potentials of this region in unknowable ways.[3]

Later that night, when I closed my eyes, I dreamed of a monk who was holding three scrolls of painted images. He wanted me to look at them, so he unrolled them for me to see. They were images of (the Taoist immortal) Lu Chunyang[4] and the bodhisattva Guanyin. The silk was all new, and the brushwork was fresh—only a wondrous hand could have drawn them. I thought that only the ancients could have achieved such marvellous subtlety. The monk said: "I have an ancient scroll of Guanyin that I can offer to you." When I unrolled it to look, sure enough, the silk was old and the image too seemed old. And there was also a boy who kept saying to me in a low voice: "This is a special vision brought on by the bodhisattva's luminous spirit—you must accept it."

When I awoke from the dream, I felt impelled to head back to Wudang. On the road I got very sick, and when I reached Xiangyang the sicknes grew more severe. My travelling companions all said: "You cannot climb the mountain." I forced myself up from my dewy seat. Suddenly there was a pure breeze: as soon as it touched my face, I abruptly felt my sickness get a little better, and inwardly I was comforted. So I accompanied the group and went up the mountain. As I walked along the road, I wasn't sick at all, but when we reached an inn, the sickness again grew serious. Everyone told me: "Stop here for a while. When the sickness gets better you can continue up the mountain—it won't be too late." I listened but I wouldn't agree. The next day I again forced myself to get up. When I reached Haohan Slope, my sickness was totally cured.

Then I went into the Yellow Gold Palace and bowed before the sage countenance of Xuanwu: I felt grateful for his spiritual assistance in making my serious illness suddenly get better. When I returned to the Pure Joy Palace, I faced Xuanwu's image and made a vow: "If I had not become a monk to learn the supreme path, then I would have fallen into uninterrupted hell for eternal ages. How strange! When I was about to cut off my hair, Guanyin appeared in the body of Xuanwu to give me spiritual assistance. Insignificant person that I am, I regret that my karma is heavy and my defilement profound. My natural potential is crude and dull: the Path cannot conquer my habits: my consciousness cannot recognize subtlety. In my poor way I have been a monk for over thirty years, without being able to pay back one part in ten thousand of Guanyin's great benevolence or your lordship's generous virtue. Yet the bodhisattva still treats me as her child and has not abandoned me. She has again appeared in a dream as a monk and bestowed on me images of the bodhisattva."

Awakening from the dream, I was deeply moved, so I have forgotten my unworthiness (and come here). I have put in proper order my priorities in becoming a monk. From beginning to end it is like images of the comings and goings of the triple world appearing in a single mirror without being obscured in the least. I want the world's people to know that Xuanwu is really a transformation body of Great Merciful Guanyin and to see that the basis for this insignificant person's aspiration for enlightenment is also generated by Xuanwu.

The virtue of Layman Chen 'Round and Pure' has also helped me profoundly. If I attain to the Path, I will deliver him first, using the samādhi of the bodhisattva's hearing, contemplation, and cultivation. Then I will not be ashamed in Guanyin's shining light.

## NOTES

1. "Guanyin alone is suitable for this region . . . " From a teaching scene in the *Śūraṅgama Sūtra:* See Luk, pp. 146-47. Sound and hearing are the special media asociated with Guanyin, the bodhisattva who observes the sounds of the world. See Mochizuki, pp. 800-07.

2. The Xiang River is a name for the Han River upstream from Xiang Yang in Hubei. About sixty miles upstream, south of the river is Mt. Wudang, which was a Taoist center with a shrine devoted to Xuanwu, lord of the dark north . . .

3. Transformation bodies: Nirmānakāya, through which Dharmakāya appears to living beings, is an expression of compassion and skill in means. "By means of Nirmāṇakāya, all the buddhas in all times perform transformations of infinite differentiation. . . . Nirmāṇakāya teach and transform living beings in all times: sometimes they show clever works, sometimes they appear to be born, sometimes they appear to attain enlightenment, sometimes they appear to show final extinction. Thus they manifest in all sorts of ways great skill in means, enabling all sentient beings to find liberation." (*Mahāyānasūtrālaṃkāra*, T 1604, p. 606c) This is the theoretical basis for the non-sectarian attitude of Buddhists: Zibo shows it in this piece by his acceptance of Taoist forms as part of the local devotional religion.

4. Lu Dongbin, also known as Chunyang 'Pure *Yang*' was a man of the capital in the Tang period who learned Taoist arts of longevity from Zhong Liquan, an immortal who had flourished under different names ever since Han and Jin times. In Tang he was on Zhong Nan Mt. and this is where Lu Chunyang received his wisdom. ZW, p. 2458.

## 9:   The Light
### (ZBJ, p. 341b)

When the light of the eyes shines on objects, at first there is no hate or love. It does not shine on sandalwood before shit. This is called the 'everywhere-equal light.' For the buddhas and ancestral teachers, through joy and anger, through sadness and happiness, there is nowhere they go that is not this fundamental everywhere-equal light. For ordinary people, amidst the clouds of affliction, it may show through for a time, but the force of habitually manifested behavior is strong, and it is immediately covered over again. Thus it is said:

> In the shadows of the colored clouds
> The spirit immortal appears,
> Holding in his hand a red gauze fan
> That covers his face:
> Look quick to see the immortal!
> Don't look at the fan in his hand!

The so-called 'clouds' and 'fan' are vexation and attachment in the pit of the five clusters (of form, sensation, conception, motivational synthesis, and consciousnes.)[1]

Thus, those who are good at progressing on the Path are able, when this light appears for a moment amidst hard to control junctures of good and evil, to set their eyes on it and see into it. They are not turned around by habitually manifested behaviors. These are called brave heroes. If the energy falters, the clouds of ignorance abruptly close in. If you only begin your meditation at this point, and struggle to dispel the clouds, it is like one man going against ten thousand—how many will be lucky enough to prevail? If when the light is revealed you wholeheartedly accept it, then the ignorance of accumulated ages at once melts away. It is like bringing Great Peace[2] to the whole world without bloodying a blade.

### NOTES

1. The five clusters: see #5, note 4.

2. Great Peace: *Tai Ping*, the name for utopian social order found in the Chinese classics like *Zhuang Zi, Lü Shi Chun Qiu*, and *Shi Ji.* ZW, p. 3416. The stress is on the peace and harmony that prevail in a well-ordered society.

# 10:   Subtle Touch
## (ZBJ, pp. 343b-c)

The Śūraṅgama Sūtra says: "Subtle touch communicates enlightenment."[1]  This saying fully opens out the fundamental light.  It's just that students' way of thinking is not subtle, so that time and again they slip by it, though it's right in front of them.

In the old days a certain head monk asked another monk: "When you hear the sound of halter bells from the other side of a wall you have broken the precept (against listening to music).  How is the precept to be upheld?"  The monk said: "(By using the sound as) a good entry road (into enlightenment)."

From this point of view, for the body, subtle touch communicates enlightenment; for the ear, subtle sound comunicates enlightenment.  If one sense faculty is this way, what sense is not?

Again: When the fourth patriarch of Zen, the great teacher Daoxin was fourteen years old, he called on the great teacher Sengcan and said: "Please teacher, give me a method of liberation."  Sengcan said: "Putting aside for a moment liberation, right now, who is binding you?"  At these words Daoxin was greatly enlightened.[2]

The ancient worthies had a saying: "Whatever you touch, whatever you encounter—all are entry roads."  Surely they did not deceive us.

### NOTES

1. "Subtle touch communicates enlightenment."  In the *Śūraṅgama Sūtra* the various sense media are revealed as avenues of enlightenment.  See Luk, pp. 121-29.

2. The biographies of the third and fourth patriarchs of Zen, Sengcan (d. 606) and Daoxin (580-651) can be found in CDL, j. 3, and in T. Cleary, *Pai-chang*, pp. 8-12.

# 11:  Sitting Meditation
## (ZBJ, pp. 343c-d)

There are three levels of quiet sitting: low-grade sitting, equanimous sitting, and sitting to add power.

Low-grade sitting is only being able to keep the tongue pressed to the roof of the mouth, the teeth firmly closed, both hands clasped with the arms at the sides, spine erect and vertical without leaning to one side.  It takes the power of faith as its leading principle.  Some recite half a verse, some recite buddha-names and mantras.[1]  The best ones have the compassionate protection of a strict teacher; the lesser ones have the help of their companions in the Dharma.  This is called low-grade sitting.

Equanimous sitting initially takes as its leading principle to see through the three sets of elements, sense organs, sense objects, and sense consciousness, to penetrate through these three sets of elements totally from beginning to end until there is no doubt.  When you are about to sit, you view your body as clouds and shadows and your mind as wind in a net.  There is no other special technique.  If you can be firm and strong, oblivion and scattering and painful stimuli are naturally peeled off.  You may sit straight through half a day or two or three days without eating or drinking, and your energy is as before.  This is called equanimous sitting.

Sitting to add power takes penetrating through to fundamental Mind as its task.  You may use the enlightenment stories[2] of the ancient worthies to shut off mental machinations and stimuli, naturally fusing into an unchanging state.  It's like carrying a mortal enemy: without your wishing it, oppressive anger blocks off space.  You persist like this until all at once the cliches of environment and person, of holy and ordinary are totally overthrown.  With this kind of willpower, energy, and strength you wear out the meditation cushion.  In a few minutes you cross over an eon, but without the thought of traversing an eon.  At this moment oblivion and scattering[3] have no place to come to rest: all of time and space as a whole are a single meditation point, extending endlessly before you filling your eyes. Suddenly the mind-ground bursts open. But you do not rejoice. Why? What you had before, you now encounter (again)—what is there that's special? This is called sitting to add power.

### NOTES

1. Recite buddha-names and mantras: see below #38, #39 and #40 and notes.

2. Enlightenment stories: The classic teaching stories of Chan tell of the 'potentials and circumstances' (*jiyuan*) of encounters leading to enlightenment. These stories were 'public cases' (*gongan*); they were used as meditation themes: hence the term *huatou*, "a saying," came to denote a meditation point.

3. Oblivion and scattering: These obstacles to enlightenment were already named styāna and vikṣepa in books like *Abhidharmakośa* and *Vijñaptimātratāsiddhi Śāstra*, according to Mochizuki, pp. 1371, 1694.

## 12:　Suffering is a Teacher
### (ZBJ, p. 343d)

For those whose natural potential is crude and rough, the Buddha's words are an obstruction. For those whose natural potential is deep, even when myriad sufferings crowd around them, they are all teachers. Hence the saying: "Use the mind well, and everywhere you touch is a basis (for enlightenment). Don't use the mind well, and everywhere is obstruction."

Before the Primordial Buddha, before the buddhas arose, there was no ground for the causal bases (of enlightenment): ultimately, who was the teacher of the Primordial Buddha? Little do you realize that suffering was the teacher. What need was there for other indicators? After the Primordial Buddha there were various indications to influence people of various potentials: they used suffering, they used bliss, they used what's neither suffering nor bliss—myriad different means. As for the Primordial Buddha, even though his natural potential was deep, unless he had been driven on by the flames of suffering, enlightenment would have been hard to develop. When his enlightenment did open up, all the causal bases (for enlightening others) flowed out from within him. This was the functioning of the Primordial Buddha's fruit of enlightenment.

Contemplate this, and all doubts and sticking points can be resolved analogously.

## 13:   Real Practitioners and Phony Adherents
### (ZBJ, pp. 344c-d)

Cultivating practice is easier than awakening to mind; awakening to mind is easier than controlling mind; controlling mind is easier than having no mind; having no mind is easier than using mind. One cannot talk about this with mere adherents and hangers-on.

Those who study Buddhism rely on Śākyamuni. Those who study Confucianism rely on Confucius. Those who study the Taoist Path rely on Laozi. Only those who awaken and penetrate to the light of mind use it freely: they dispense with all dependencies, and take their own stand on open ground, like the lion king strolling back and forth, springing forward or stopping still at will, totally independent.

For example, when head monk Ding came from Linji,[1] someone asked: "How do Zen men investigate to the end?" Ding immediately grabbed ahold of him and threw him off the bridge. Some of his travelling companions understood him. Ding said: "If not for this old frozen snot, Zen men would indeed investigate to the end!" Ding can be called one who used it freely.

In transcending the world, such functioning is called Buddhism; in managing the world it is called Confucianism; in nurturing life it is called Taoism.

Mere adherents of these (three teachings) are like merchant barges with no motive power of their own, that depend on the power of others. They advertize themselves under the signboard of such-and-such literary academy, scriptural studies temple, or official training school in order to cheat and deceive the ignorant. Few are those who are not swayed in the face of their reputations. But if they happen to meet a real master, not only don't they dare to boast of the labels they have arrogated for themselves, but they hide them without delay. Alas! Such fellows stand with their heads to the sky, angrily frowning and glaring, full of lofty talk and hollow theories. Who among them does not deem himself an outstanding disciple of the sages? If one morning they bump into a guy without a face who taps them lightly with the hole-less hammer,[2] their eyes show confusion, and they cannot fend them off.

How can we expect people like this to be able to understand the meaning of the four degrees of difficulty (involved in cultivating practice, controlling mind, being mindless, and using mind)?

### NOTES

1. Head Monk Ding: He studied under Linji in the ninth century. His story is in BCR 32, in the commentary to the case.

2. A hole-less hammer: a hammer head with no hole in which to fasten a handle. Used in Chan to refer to the expression of the ineffable by the worthy teachers. See BCR 14.

## 14:  Perception and Dream
### (ZBJ, pp. 345a-b)

When awake everyone sees form where there is form and not where there is not. This is the usual situation, for the whole world. When dreaming, everyone sees form where there is no form, and does not see form where there is form. This too is the common situation for the whole world.

It is only those who comprehend the Path who use the situation of seeing form where there is no form while dreaming, to prove the falsity of seeing form where "there is form" while awake. It is as clear as sun and stars: what further confusion is there?

## 15: The Face of Enlightenment
### (ZBJ, p. 345b)

A monk asked: "When Linji returned from seeing Dayu, how did Huangbo know that he had penetrated the great affair?"[1]

The Teacher said: When those who are cold get a drink of wine, it becomes spring on their faces. When the hungry get food, their spirits radiate joy. How much the more so for one drunk on the supreme elixir!

### NOTES

1. Linji Yixuan (d. 867) was the ancestral teacher of one of the main streams of Chan. The story of his encounter with Dayu is in the commentary to Case 11 of the BCR. His biography is in CDL j. 12 and BCR, pp. 253-57. Huangbo (d. 850) was Linji's main teacher, who had sent him to Dayu.

## 16: Subjectivity
### (ZBJ, pp. 346a-b)

The ancients were concerned about the way the world's people make food and drink and sex their chief desires. They wish to correct this, little knowing that they were worrying about only one side of the problem, not worrying about both sides. If not for the knowing subject, there would be no basis for taking pleasure in food and drink and sex. To worry about the objects of knowledge without worrying about the knowing subject is to ignore the parallelism.

The knowing subject is hard to smash, because habits have gelled into second nature—it is like oil put into flour. Unless you can penetrate through to fundamental mind, and use the luminous selfless one to deal with habits, the oil will never be taken out of the flour.

These days those whom the world knows as expounders of the Path do not realize that the knowing subject is a thief. They feed and foster it inordinately and mightily help it grow. The so-called selfless luminous one remains forever dormant and is never unfurled. What's worse, they accept the knowing subject as their master, and consider that it sees reality-nature, that it is innate awareness (*liang zhi*).[1] Alas! They are calling the slave the free one: what could be worse?

The awareness of an ant can encompass the area of a mustard seed; the awareness of a giant bird can encompass thousands of miles. Nevertheless, when we investigate that they proceed from, though it may be called great or small, the subjectivity is the same.

Thus it is said: "Split open an atom of dust, and all the scriptures in the universe issue forth."[2] Unless you have heard of the path, you cannot do this. For example, dragons perceive with spirit, snakes perceive with the eye, oxen perceive with the nose. The sense organ varies but the perceiving is not different. (The limitations of) the knowing subject can be deduced analogously.

## NOTES

1. *Liang zhi*: A key term in the philosophy of Wang Yangming (1472-1527), most influential Confucian philosopher of the later Ming. The concept derives from Mencius, where *liang zhi* has the sense of 'innate knowledge' from which social norms are derived (*Mencius*, 7 B 15). Yangming gave this idea fresh impetus in the early part of the sixteenth century. Here is his view from *Chuan Xi Lu* (complete works, vol. 2, p. 46): "Mencius said, 'The Path is like a great highway— how could it be hard to know? People's defect lies in not following it.' (6 B 2) Innate abilities and innate knowledge are the same in ignorant men and women and in sages, it's just that only the sages can

extend/bring into play their innate knowledge (*zhi liang zhi*), but ignorant men and women cannot. This is what separates ignorant and sage. . . . At difficult turning points innate knowledge is like a compass and ruler for drawing circles and making measurements. . . ."

2. "Split open an atom . . ." The *Hua Yan* shows myriads of bodhisattvas showing within each and every atom all objects in all worlds to teach all sentient beings in timely fashion. See T. Cleary, *Entry into the Inconceivable*, pp. 4-5.

# 17: Blind Views of Buddhism
## (ZBJ, pp. 346c-347c)

Recently the Buddhist Teaching has been greatly troubled. The trouble is not due to demons or outsiders: the trouble lies in seven major faults of blind teachers and disciples.

The first fault: The opinion that enlightenment is only possible by means of the enlightenment stories of the ancient worthies of the Zen family, that enlightenment has nothing to do with the scriptural vehicle.

I ask you: What about Zen master An, who was enlightened while reading the refutations in the Śūraṅgama Sūtra? What about Yongjia, who was enlightened when he read the Vimala-kīrti Sūtra?[1] What about Zen master Su of Pu An[2] and Ying Zhaowu,[3] who were both enlightened from reading the Hua Yan treatises? If you think that you can only be enlightened by the enlightenment stories of Zen, but not by the scriptures, isn't this a great error?

The second fault: The opinion that because knowledge and reason block the gate of spontaneous awakening, and the Path is not entered via the eyes and ears, it is necessary to shut everything off, waiting until 'the kernel pops in the cold ashes,' in order to illuminate the great matter, comprehend everything correctly, and attain once and for all.

I ask you: In today's world, among monks and laypeople, who even possesses knowledge and reason? If you can actually point out one or half a one, I would surely cherish him whether he was enlightened or not. I'm afraid, though, that there wouldn't be many (who are really knowledgeable or reasonable).

One day Wang Anshi[4] asked Zen master Yuan of Jiangshan:[5] "Could I hear the special transmission outside the verbal teachings?" Yuan said: "You have something blocking you. For now rely on the rich spiritual roots of the ocean of the scriptures. In one or two more births, you will be qualified (for what you ask)."

People these days are far from equal to Wang Anshi, yet before they can even crawl, they study running. Isn't this a great error?

The third fault: The opinion that, compared to studying Zen or reading the scriptures, it is easy to recite the buddha-name to seek birth in the Pure Land—this is the surest play.

I ask you: Can a person with a defiled mind be born in the Pure Land? Can a person with a pure mind? Can a person with mind half pure and half defiled? Are people with wholly pure minds born there? If a person with a defiled mind could be born in the Pure Land, this would be a contradiction between name and reality, a dissociation of cause and effect. As for the idea that a person with mind half pure and half defiled can be born in the Pure Land, I have heard a saying of the ancient worthies: "If a person facing death has the least bit of emotional consciousness thinking of this world, he cannot be born in the Pure Land." As for those whose minds are wholly pure, wherever they go is the Pure Land, and whatever they do is Pure Land conduct. Thus, is it not a great error to think that the one act of reciting the buddha-name can surpass studying Zen and reading the scriptures?

The fourth fault: There are some blind roosters who hear true roosters crowing and false roosters crowing and imitate them all, making all sorts of noises. Their opinion is that 'the movement of thought goes against the basic essence,' that 'calculating thought descends into plans for living in the house of delusion, and even more so if there are words.'

I ask you: Is such perceptive consciousness understanding or is it action? If it is understanding, what's wrong with the movement of thought? Why find fault with calculating thought? Only after the ancients had five pecks of rice thoroughly cooked could they reply with a turning word without going against the basic essence: then all the great elders of Zen approved their penetrating enlightenment. It is also said: "Ponder it, think about it! Comprehend the spirit and what's not the spirit. Then the mind will open and be illuminated." So what's the harm of calculating thought? Furthermore, Guanyin influences and transforms all beings with the three wisdoms of hearing, contemplation, and practice.[6] How could you one-sidedly maintain that thought is a defect? Isn't this a great error?

The fifth fault: The opinion that human life is never without desire; that only the sages are able to curb desire and not follow it. There are also those who indulge desire without any restraint, (who claim to be) relying on the seeds of wisdom of many births (to eventually lead them to realization). When they get a little garbled knowledge of the scriptures, they view everything as empty, and think that the inner truth achieved by the ancients did not go beyond this. (Their attitude is:) since fundamentally there is nothing, what need is there for special study? But amidst the winds of adverse and favorable circumstances, they are blown back and forth, and cannot act the master in the least.

I ask you: When the ancients could see, they could act. In this brainlessness of yours, you can see, but you cannot act. Really you haven't even seen it in a dream. Do you dare to feel no shame as you blunder around with such big talk, vainly incurring painful consequences? Isn't this a great error?

The sixth fault: There are people in the 'Three Teachings' without a fixed view of any of them. Studying Confucianism without mastering it, they abandon Confucianism to study Buddhism. Studying Buddhism without mastering it, they abandon Buddhism to study Taoism. Studying Taoism without mastering it, they flow into the marginal schools—there is nowhere they do not go.

I ask you: Have you actually reached the realm of Confucius and Mencius no not? If you have, you certainly would not act this way. If you haven't even mastered Confucianism, how can you study Buddhism? If you haven't mastered Buddhism, what spare time is there to study Taoism?

There is another kind of person, who thinks that first among the principles of Buddhism is the crux of righteousness vs. gain. But even this they do not see clearly, much less the Path of the sages. Moreover their writings are broad in scope but vague: you can never find their boundaries. Better that each holds his own Path and turns away from things he doesn't understand.

I ask you: Have you awakened to the mind of enlightenment or not? If you had awakened to the buddha mind, your mind would naturally have no doubts and no regrets and you would have entered into certainty. Now you are not ashamed of your natural potential being shallow and crude, yet you are doubting the Buddha's scriptures. Isn't this a great error?

The seventh fault: (The opinion that Buddhists today) whether they are at home or have left home, when compared to the monks and laymen of the Tang and Song, are as difference as the heavens and the abyss. The people of Tang and Song times, like Pei Xiu[7] and Su Shi,[8] had insight into both Zen and the scriptural teachings: sometimes with a phrase or a verse they extolled our Path like moonlight shining on a carriage. Their light cannot be hidden: its brilliance vies with the sun of enlightenment.

(I reply:) Even among us, some have matched them. Even memorial inscriptions and prefaces to scriptures, whatever their length or brevity, can only reach accord with the sūtras if there is true attainment of the buddha mind.

In this dynasty, I wouldn't say there have been none since Song Lian[9] who could extol our Path with words, but I daresay there have been few. It is because the gentlemen of Tang and Song consorted with people outside official circles: together they were able to transcend sentiment and detach from views, smash the net of conventionalism, and relegate gain and loss and glory and disgrace to a place among the sky flowers. Mind to mind they reflected on each other like light going back and forth between two mirrors. Therefore the style they bequeathed still has its sharpness.

Alas! Not being able themselves to adhere to this style, later people have sought the Path by means of sentiments. This is what is called 'heading south to go north.' Yet seeking the Path by departing from sentiments is called 'seeking the water apart from the waves.' If a person has another road between these two on which to come forth, and he doesn't infringe on the prohibition (against dualistic biases), I guarantee that in time he will awaken to the Path even without studying Zen or reading the scriptures. If you cannot establish a firm standpoint between the two (extremes of indulging or suppressing sentiments), better to be a perpetually travelling rice-eater.

These days some monks and lay people approach spiritual teachers with the attitude of judging and assessing the teacher before they have seen him: they figure that a certain teacher does not go beyond this, that another teacher is no more than that. Once this attitude is born, even if the Tathāgata arose again, not even he could benefit these seekers, so how could anyone else do so? Generally, approaching spiritual teachers may be likened to picking peaches: there is no time to be concerned with whether the tree is crooked or straight, all that matters is the fineness of the peaches. This being so, is it not a great error to approach spiritual teachers stubbornly using sentimental consciousness to seek the Path?

I have given a rough account of these seven errors, unmindful of what the outstanding worthies, monk or lay, may think.

Nevertheless, these seven errors are purified elixir, as well as being poisons. If you make good use of them, poisons have never not been elixir. If you do not make good use of it, elixir has never not been poison.

Again, I ask you: Before a single thought is born, where will you put these seven errors? After a thought is born, where will you put them? If anyone can tell, I will someday be picking up shoes and fetching the water pitcher for him. If you cannot tell, don't be too crude, or you'll make other people who are clear-eyed laugh at you.

## NOTES

1. Yongjia (d. 713) was a man who had deeply studied the canonical teachings and the Tiantai philosophy and reached independent enlightenment. He stayed one night with the Sixth Patriarch and got his approval. See CDL, j. 5. His works the *Song of Enlightenment* (T 2014) and the *Yongjia Collection* (T 2013) were read down through the ages in Chan circles.

2. Yinsu of Pu An (1115-1169) was in the Yangqi branch of the Linji stream. See ZG, p. 57.

3. Ying Zhaowu, also known as Hongying of Bao Feng, lived in the eleventh century and was a pupil of the great Chan master Huanglong Huinan (d. 1069). See ZG, p. 83.

4. Wang Anshi was the leader of an attempt at political reforms from 1069-1076 aimed at strengthening the power of the central state. See Cai Meibiao, pp. 27-33.

5. Zanyuan of Jiangshan told Wang Anshi that his affinity for the Path was blocked by mental turmoil caused by th press of duty, his preoccupation with state affairs, and his propensity to be easily angered. See ZG, p. 548.

6. Guanyin and the three wisdoms: See #8, note 1.

7. Pei Xiu (797-870) was a high official with contacts in Buddhist circles: he was a pupil of Huangbo Xiyun. See CDL, j. 12.

8. Su Shi (1037-1101, *jinshi* 1056) was a brilliant writer and cultural leader of the Song period, who also held high office and maintained links with Buddhists. See Cyril Clark, *The Prose-Poetry of Su Tung-po*, pp. 3-13, 37-39.

9. Song Lian (1310-1381) was a Confucian scholar and teacher from Zhejiang who became one of Zhu Yuanzhang's chief advisors from 1360 onwards. He was well acquainted with Buddhism and sympathetic towards it. See *Dictionary of Ming Biography*, pp. 1225-31.

# 18:  Approaching the Treasury of Light
### (ZBJ, pp. 349a-b)

"The Bhagavān entered into the treasury of the great light of spiritual powers, and with non-dual accord, made all the pure lands appear, along with hundreds of thousands of great bodhisattvas and mahāsattvas. Their names were: Mañjuśrī, Samantabhadra, Universal Eye, Diamond Treasury, Maitreya, Pure Wisdom, Lord of Awesome Virtue, Discriminator of Sounds, Purifier of Karmic Obstructions, Universal Enlightenment, Perfect Enlightenment, Leader of the Good and so on. Together they entered the treasury of the great light of spiritual powers."[1] Ah!

This treasury of great light—could it be that only the Bhagavān and the great bodhisattvas have it, while all the sentient beings have no share in it? Nevertheless, sentient beings miss the selfless luminous awareness and instead accept the egoistic awareness that clings to objects as their own minds. For this reason (the treasury of light is like) the precious treasure in the poor girl's house or the bright jewel in the garment of the destitute boy—it is present, but they cannot make use of it.

All sentient beings witness perfect enlightenment—these are the words of our Bhagavān. By means of this endowment the ancients easily experienced (enlightenment). Zen master Wen of Zhen Jing[2] called them stinking slaves for letting words and principles obstruct their own fundamental mind, for still doubting the Buddha's words and not believing them, and for falsely altering the scriptures. Thus we can know that he was enlightened.

Thus it is said: "If you are not involved in emotional interpretations, it appears before you right on the spot." When the roads of ordinary and sage are cut off, then where will you put the so-called Bhagavān and all the great bodhisattvas?

You once visited me at Long Pine Monastery and vowed to recite the Sūtra of Complete Enlightenment. First you read it and read it until you had memorized it. Once you had memorized it, you could recite it without depending on the text.

You were able to advance upstream: at first you relied on the text, then you put aside the text and memorized it, so that you could recite it from memory.

If by reciting it you can accurately master it, if by accurately mastering it you can enter into it, then is there really any distinction between the so-called treasury of the great light of spiritual powers and the Bhagavān and all the great bodhisattvas when you encounter them?

If you can pick them out, then nothing stands in the way of your suddenly encountering them later on amidst flowing waters and wilderness clouds, in the city of the peach blossom spring.[3] Then you will be able to discuss the flowing phrases of the old fellow Leader of the Good.

How much time can there be for us? If the treasury of the light of spiritual powers is completely buried at the gate of sound and form, then better not to have been born. Work hard at this and experience it!

### NOTES

1. "The Bhagavān entered . . . " Bhagavān is an epithet of Buddha. This is the opening scene of the Sūtra of Complete Enlightenment, T 842, pp. 913a-b. The treasury of the great light of spiritual powers is the pure ground of enlightenment of all beings, where body and mind are quiescent, the everywhere equal fundamental reality.

2. Kewen of Zhen Jing (1025-1102) studied in the Huanglong school of Linji Chan. See WDHY, j. 17.

3. Peach Blossom Spring: Traditionally, an idyllic place of refuge from the strife and chaos of the world, as in the poem of Tao Qian. See Hightower, *The Poetry of T'ao Chi'ien.*

# 19.  Causal Conditions for Enlightenment
### (ZBJ, pp. 350a-b)

The poor long for wealth. The wealthy long for noble rank. The nobility long for security and ease. Those secure and at ease long for immortality.

Little do they realize that from longing comes having birth; from birth comes riches and nobility, poverty and low station, security and ease, and also all forms of existence and suffering, continuing inexhaustibly. Therefore, if you want to cross the sea of suffering, you must take the boat of having no longings. Only then can you climb up onto that other shore.

But longing cannot nullify itself—in order to nullify longing you must hear the Path. The Path cannot be heard by itself—here too you must depend on causal conditions to draw you to it: then it will be heard. Causal conditions are truly the mother of all the buddhas, the teachers who sustain sentient beings.

Taking marks of goodness as the causal basis means, for example, beholding the countenance of a virtuous person and having one's meanness and pettiness spontaneously dissolve. Taking sound as the causal basis means, for example, the mind ground opening through under the impact of a single word. Other things too can be taken as the causal basis: the teachings of the sages, great enlightened teachers, good friends and Dharma companions, adverse situations, favorable situations. Or else, as a causal basis you can advance diligently being brave and bold, peeling off your skin for paper, splitting your bones for a pen, drawing blood for ink, to copy the scriptures of the Great Vehicle. Thus it is said: "The seed of enlightenment arises from causal conditions."

Though all these kinds of causal conditions are aids to hearing the Path, the most excellent is the last: drawing blood for ink and copying the scriptures. Living beings cling tenaciously to bodily form. If a tiny mosquito bites them, they cannot overcome their annoyance: they will try to brush it away, and won't stop until they do. Much less can they steadfastly endure the pain of pricking the finger with a sharp needle until the blood flows and the mind feels the shock. It will scarcely be easy to see this excellent cause through to the end, unless your longstanding mind of faith is firm and true, and your conscious perspective goes beyond the ordinary crowd.

The venerable Guanxiu[1] of Tang said of the Zen master
Chuyun copying the Lotus Sūtra in blood:

> He cut his skin to make the blood flow—
> How painful indeed!
> He did it to copy the nine-part Spirit
>     Mountain text.
> When the flow from his ten fingers had dried,
> The text was complete in seven scrolls.
> Among later seekers of the Dharma,
> There were none like him!

You should recite this poem with feeling several dozen
times: then the clinging to the body will get lighter by itself.
Once clinging to the body has lightened, this scripture (you
intend to copy) is only some five thousand words—how could
it be hard to write it out?

To Layman Fadeng on writing out the Diamond Sūtra
in blood.

### NOTES

1. Guanxiu (832-912) was a man from Jinhua in Zhejiang with
many contacts among monks and in polite society. He studied with
the Chan teacher Shishuang Qingzhu. He was well-known as the
author of the collection of poetry *Chan Yue Ji/Zen Moon Collection*.
See ZG, p. 176.

## 20:   The Light of the Buddhas
### (ZBJ, p. 350b-c)

When I read Zhi Qian's translation of the Amida Sūtra,[1]
I first came to know that there are differences in the
scope of the light that comes from the heads of the various
buddhas. There are lights that reach seventy feet, lights that
reach a mile, lights that reach a hundred miles, and so on up
to lights that reach tens of millions of miles. Only the light
from the head of Amida is most excellent, being infinite.

On Mt. She, behind Qi Xia Temple, is Thousand Buddhas Peak.[2] The peak has a cliff honeycombed with niches containing buddha-images: the galleries wind back and forth set out in many tiers. The sizes of the buddha-images vary from large to small.

In the past the Qi courtier Ming Sengshao[3] invited the Zen teacher Fadu to lecture on the Sūtra of the Buddha of Infinite Light. Heaven was moved to rain down flowers all around. In a dream the courtier beheld Buddha's countenance: when he awoke he ordered images to be carved into the mountain according to what he had seen in the dream—many many images were made. Before the project was completed, the courtier died; his son, who was prefect of Linyi, continued his father's intention and had it completed.

From the Qi dynasty to the Yuan dynasty was almost a thousand years. During this time temples were built and ruined, Buddhism was (repeatedly) built up and ruined, all due to combinations of circumstances.

When Wushu of the Jin[4] occupied Mt. She with his troops, he was about to do battle, and he prayed to the Buddha for mysterious aid. When he lost the battle, he gave an order to his commanders saying: "Since Buddha did not bring me luck, but instead helped the rebels, Buddha must be a rebel. We must destroy him to wipe away this outrage!" Thus all the images set in the cliff-face niches, whether great or small, met with destruction. In some cases fragments of bodies or heads remain, or faces or arms smashed and lying there jumbled together. Those who see this are saddened by it.

Although I am not quick-witted, I dare to rely on the loving spiritual aid of the Tathāgata. With a blessing received in the private room of Zen-uncle Cang, with whom I formerly shared a hermitage, I vowed to repair this site. One of the Zen-uncle's "grandsons," named Haiyin, heard of my words, and vowed to volunteer himself to undertake this project.

Alas! The Qi courtier served the buddhas; Wushu tore them down. What served the buddhas was mind; what tore them down was also mind. Used well, the light (of mind) flows through ten thousand generations. In the opposite case, the evil fills space: the evil repute will not be wiped away until space itself is destroyed. We must be careful with the light of mind!

Moreover, outside of mind there is no buddha, outside of buddha there is no mind. When sentiments of 'mind' and 'buddha' dissolve, the eternal light is revealed alone, and the accepting mind gives its own sanction. This light has a seventy-foot manifestation and it has a hundred million foot manifestation. It also has a manifestation that reaches to infinite lands. It is not that the paths of the buddhas are different: it is that the vows they have undertaken with causal conditions are not the same.

Haiyin has come before me, I who am a man of east, west, south and north, I who come and go with no fixed pattern. So I have provisionally written this to bequeath to him, that he may exert himself in this work.

## NOTES

1. Zhi Qian: a Central Asian born in China, he worked at Jianye (Nanking) in the mid-third century translating Buddhist texts, among them the Vimalakīrti Sūtra (T 474) and the Amida Sūtra (T 362).

2. Mt. She is in Jiangsu. Linyi is a city in southeast Shandong. In the twelfth century this was a zone of military conflict between the Jin to the north and the Southern Song.

3. Ming Sengshao lived in the fifth century: his brothers were military governors under the Liu Song regime, and the family remained prominent under the Qi regime which replaced it in 479. ZW, p. 6429.

4. Wushu was the fourth son of the founder of the Jurchen Jin dynasty, Akuta of the Wenyan clan (d. 1123). After taking Kaifeng, the Song capital, in 1126, the Jin in subsequent years established their rule over north China and continued to put military pressure on the Southern Song. Wushu was known for his prowess in war, and led many campaigns against the Song. ZW, p. 1262.

# 21: Entering Through the Senses
## (ZBJ, pp. 351c-d)

With One Mind unborn, being and nothingness are not in opposition—much less is there a perceiver.

Even so, once one mind is born, the six sense faculties are already provided. It is not possible to have entry (into enlightenment) by abandoning these. Therefore when the perfected people expound the Teaching, they may explain it with the tongue, so that it can be entered via the ears, or they may explain it with the body, so that it can be entered via the eye. Using these and all the sense faculties, according to the surroundings they open up its subtlety, without constant pattern they take in its marvel.

This being so, all things are the marks of the Tathāgata's long broad tongue:[1] sad songs, deep feelings, swearing and chiding, thorn forests and trees of beauty, gowns and caps, rites and music, drums and flutes, drinking, eating, sex, right and wrong, good and evil, the clash of weapons, the formal dance, silent misty forests, noisy urban squares. Whether one has entry or does not, depends on how one hears (Buddha's tongue in all these forms).

Wan Li *gui-si* (1593), spring, third month, eleventh day.

> The evening sun is on the peaks
> Stove smoke frozen blue
> The empty hall is like a mirror
> The mind's eye clear and steady

Just then Mr. Kai came in, made a formal bow, and stood (to report) that the monk in charge of vegetarian feasts had spoken of expounding the Dharma with the body, so the eyes can hear it, and expounding the Dharma with the tongue, so the ears can see it. Unconsciously I felt at ease and very happy and said: "Indeed it can be said that my disciple knows how to talk!"

On this occasion I've taken up the brush to write this down, in order to enlarge upon its meaning.

To Daokai

### NOTES

1. The Tathāgata's long broad tongue: Originally one of the thirty-two auspicious marks of the Buddha, this came to be taken in a broader sense as symbolic of the universality and infinite multiformity of the teaching of enlightenment. ZG, 805, quotes Wuzu Fayan (d. 1114), the teacher of Yuanwu, 'grandfather' of Dahui: "All the buddhas of the ten directions, the six generations of patriarchs, and all the world's enlightened teachers all share this tongue. Only if you recognize this tongue will you be capable of great emptying out. Then you will say that mountains, rivers, and the great earth are Buddha, grasses and trees and forests are Buddha. If you have not recognized this tongue, it justs amounts to petty emptying, and you go on deceiving yourself."

# 22:   A Dream at Daybreak
## (ZBJ, pp. 351c-d)

The sages established laws by which to prevent treachery and wrongdoing. The ancestral teachers devised guiding principles with which to ward off demons and outsiders.

Thus, whether ordinary or sage, if you do not move out from within these traps (of treachery, wrongdoing, delusion, and alienation from reality), even if you have some subtle perceptions, it is not the correct basis (for enlightenment). Therefore Zen master Hui of Yantou[1] said: "Just comprehend the guiding principles: fundamentally there is no real Dharma."

The years have come and gone—Buddha is far away. True students rarely appear. Everywhere the others flock together and follow the crowd, babbling in confusion. If they encounter an adept, they bring up a section of the Great Ming Code and investigate the crime according to the bribe: even in you were an ancient Buddha come again, you would still have to pay the amount. So much the worse for devils of small faculties!

Although it is so, tell me, how will you understand the ultimate in terms of words?

Joy in heaven has an end
Suffering among humans is inexhaustible
A hundred years is like a dream at daybreak
Not depending on waking up to be empty

### NOTES

1. Yantou (828-887) was one of the great Chan teachers, a successor to Deshan Xuanjian (781-867) and a fellow student with Xuefeng Yicun. See BCR Cases 51 and 66, and biography in CDL, j. 16 and BCR, pp. 455-56.

## 23: Discipline That Liberates[1]
### (ZZ-ZBJ, pp. 352d-353a)

Food and sex are the great desires of human beings. Therefore, if people can curb the great desires, then they can be told about the path of supreme enlightenment.

But the great desires are harder to control than poisonous dragons or wild tigers. Accordingly, near the end of his life, the Buddha was asked by Ānanda, "After the Buddha's demise, what can the monks, nuns, laymen, and laywomen take as their teacher?" The Tathāgata commanded: "After my decease, all those who are my disciples should take the comprehensive discipline of being liberated from all attachments (*prātimokṣa*) as your teacher. If you can do this, then it will be no different from when I was staying in the world."[2]

Viewing things according to this, since we are Buddha's disciples, how could we dare not to uphold *prātimokṣa*? These days we are far from the time of Buddha. It is not only the monks in remote hideaways who do not follow methods of discipline—even in famous Buddhist centers they don't know what *prātimokṣa* is. How sad!

When one's mind is pure and clean, the root of discipline is fundamentally cleansed. When one's mind is empty and still, the water of concentration is fundamentally cleared.

When one's mind is thoroughly illuminated, the light of wisdom is round and full.[3]

A moment of neglect, an uncalled for forced awareness—what we call inherent discipline, concentration, and wisdom are lost in delusion and become craving, anger, and ignorance. From then on, from birth to death, from death to birth, death after death, birth after birth, they are wrapped up continuously in the web of their deeds, rising and falling without constancy, wearing scales or shells or feathers or fur, a deva's cap or human's clothes. The myriad kinds of suffering and pleasure are all called 'ignorance.' Thus the saying: "If you submissively follow ignorance, you fall into the various states of being. If you do not submissively follow, the states of being are cut off." This being so, then ignorance and wisdom are like one and the same finger being curled up or extended.

What I get all comes from my own mind—how could I be using some other power? It depends on whether or not the person in question is willing. If they themselves actually agree to develop the mind of enlightenment, even very ignorant people, who just know to drink when thirsty, eat when hungry, and feel attracted to the opposite sex—once they achieve the willing mind, then they can use this to discover that body does not exist and mind is only a name. When we are liberated in respect to body and mind, adverse and favorable situations and all the myriad differences all emit the light of our own mind. At this point, there is no place to put 'wisdom' much less 'ignorance'!

Thus do I know that there are no ignorant people or wise people—it's just a matter of whether or not they develop the mind (willing to learn enlightenment). Thus even knowledgeable people, if they have not developed the willing mind, are no different from oxen or horses.

To those present here I say: "You should no longer discuss what you have done in the past. Since you have pledged yourselves (to be Buddhist monks) you must together honor the Buddha's commands. Refuse contact with women and don't let them enter the monastery. When women do not enter the monastery, the fragrance of virtue will be pure and far-reaching and the streams and stones will emit light. The dead will find birth in good places and the living will get all good fortune. If these are the slightest violation of Buddha's commands, the dead will fall further and the living will perish.

Let each and every one of you present here get to know good and bad: you should take *prātimokṣa* as your teacher. Don't be lazy, don't leave a legacy of suffering for later.

> To the assembly of monks at
> Jue Shan Si

### NOTES

1. Discipline that Liberates: The term for discipline, *prātimokṣa* means 'thorough-going liberation', 'liberation in every particular.' SY, p. 919. The *prātimoksa* regulations are laid out in the second half of the Brahmajāla Sūtra (T 21), known as the Prātimokṣa Sūtra. Soothill, pp. 266, 354.

2. "Near the end of his life, the Buddha was asked by Ānanda ... " This is a scene in the *Mahāparinirvāṇa Sūtra* (T 374, T 375). See Mochizuki, pp. 4275, 4708.

3. Discipline, concentration, and wisdom: These are the traditional 'three studies' of Buddhism. SY, p. 789.

## 24: How and When to Travel
### (ZBJ, p. 354c-d)

You wish to travel to other places. This is really a good thing. Tracing it back into ancient times, of all those who became great vessels (of the Dharma) in their own time, not one did not come forth from travels on foot. If one does not travel all over to the gates of enlightened teachers to undergo forging under their hammers and tongs, it is impossible to become a vessel.

Nevertheless, you need not always travel and never stay

anywhere, nor should you always stay put and never travel. Just go when you should go and stay when you should stay.

When should you go? Maybe when you are eating your fill and dwelling idly, when you are indulging your sentiments and giving free rein to your desires. How could you stay and not go?

When should you stay? Maybe when you have met a teacher with stringent methods, a spiritual friend who lives up to the true correct Path. How could you go and not stay?

From your viewpoint, you consider the confusion of worldly entanglements incompatible with the Buddha Dharma: you plan to abandon them and seek elsewhere. Little do you know that Buddha Dharma and worldly things are extras that have nothing at all to do with your own lot. Better face the confusion, turn your head around and reverse your brain, and see what it ultimately is. Don't ward it off as worldly entanglement and don't grasp the understanding of it as Buddha Dharma. After a long time you will suddenly have insight. Then the work is redoubled.

Though you wish to go travelling on foot, if your seeking mind does not cease, if thoughts linked to objects tangle in confusion, today in one district, tomorrow in another, running south and running north, eyes staring hungrily, mind racing on and on until your hair turns white—you will never succeed.

You must press down the clouds, and cast aside your life. As you pass through difficulties and dangers, your face must be like cast iron. As you encounter pleasure and joy, your mind's purpose must be made of pure steel. Mind doesn't reach objects, objects don't reach mind. If you are like this you are in some measure qualified to travel on foot.

## 25: The Value of Adversity
### (ZBJ, pp. 358c-d)

The workings of mind have no constancy: controlling them is up to the person. If you control mind with the power of the Path, you do not pay attention to success and profit. If you control mind by means of success and profit, you do not pay attention to humanity and righteousness. Tracing back what they start from, though they proceed differently, neither the power of the Path nor success and profit is beyond one's own mind. The divergence is in what the will is placed on.

When the power of the Path controls the mind, everything is a stepping-stone, even being robbed and mistreated. When success and profit control the mind, everything is a cause for alarm, even glory and honor. When causes of alarm disturb the mind, the spirit is always troubled: all the more so when one is robbed or mistreated. Thus a person studying the Path considers it the best luck to be in unwished for situations. If one does not awaken amidst this great good luck, but rather floats along pursuing objects, this is called dimming the mind. A person whose mind is dimmed, even if in daily contact with sages and saints, is no different from a blind man who thinks it's the dead of night even though the bright sun is above his head.

Generally, if you just don't deceive mind, mind of itself is luminous and wise. Using the luminous and wise mind, when you are placed in unwished for situations, they are like remnants of snow naturally melting away in spring. It doesn't take crashing thunder splitting the earth open to disperse them.

The Book of Poetry says: "The stone of another mountain can be used to cut jade."[1] If you use jade to cut jade forming a vessel is exceedingly difficult, because both are smooth, and rubbing them together has no effect. Thus, when you are placed in a desirable situation, mind and situation are both forgotten. Since you forget, you lose awareness. Even if you have a strict teacher or spiritual friend to give you illuminating instructions most conscientiously, you nevertheless foster the habit of overfamiliarity. Once the habit of familiarity is formed, you are like a favorite child who feels no awe toward his parents. If the mind has no awe, where does respect come from? Without respect, without awe, how can there be any benefit?

Thus it is said: "Adverse situations are a spear in your face. Favorable situations are an arrow in the back of your head." The spear in your face is easy to dodge. The arrow in the back of your head is hard to defend against.

Moreover, the worldly way is more and more in decline. For a long time the tradition of enlightened teachers has been decrepit and moribund. Strict teachers and spiritual friends are not easy to meet. If you are able to use unwished for situations as your teachers and stepping-stones, wherever you go there are strict teachers and spiritual friends.

Emotional consciousness floats and sinks—the four elements are added on and stripped off. If you can let the light of wisdom appear alone, empty and peaceful, you return to the source. Though the old sticking points are there, if you do not encourage them, how can they do harm?

*To Zhongfu when sick*

NOTES

1. "The stone of another mountain can be used to cut jade." This is from the classic of poetry, *Shi Jing*, #184, the last line of the second stanza.

## 26:  Adaptable Compassion
### (ZBJ, p. 359b)

Generally people pay back their parents' virtue by making offerings of food on prescribed occasions. But they are only increasing their black karma. Worldly conventional people are benighted and blind: it is always hard to explain the true principle to them.

Temporarily going along with their customs and practices to make them happy, the sage worthies realize that their habits are not easily changed. Provisionally floating and sinking along with them, the sages use inner truth to cut away their sentiments, working in the shadows, secretly taming and tempering them. After long effort, the power is sufficient, and their habits change by themselves. Those who are undergoing the tempering are oblivious to why it is so. Thus the sages share the vicissitudes of social forms. If they didn't rejoice at what the conventional people celebrate, if they didn't offer condolences when the conventional people mourn, this would mean bitter feelings against the sages.

Nevertheless, if the sages did not use the light of supreme compassion to illuminate the dark confusion of conventional people, they would be stuck there and be forever relegated among the unsalvageable. How could this be the fundamental mental state of these people? If we want to illuminate their dark confusion, for the living it is best that we purify our own conduct, and for the dead it is simplest and most beneficial that we recite Viśvābhu Buddha's verse.[1]

### NOTES

1. Viśvābhu's Verse: see #7 and notes.

## 27: The Process of Delusion
### (ZBJ, pp. 365c-366a)

Before joy and anger take shape, inherent nature is originally complete. Once joy and anger have taken shape, if what is generated does not go wrong, and does not go against what's there before it's generated, this is called 'harmony.' If there is the slightest inclination to bias, this is called 'disharmony.' With harmony good fortune gathers. With disharmony, ten thousand faults arise. When good fortune gathers, you share the same bloodline with the buddhas and ancestral teachers and sages. When then thousand faults arise, you share the practices of petty men and all kinds of bad types.

When habitual practices are deep-rooted, they are hard to remold even with heaven and earth as the furnace, *yin* and *yang* as the fuel, a whirlwind for a bellows, and the creator's power. Thus the Buddha used the water of emptiness to wash them away.

The means by which sentient beings go wrong is no more than desire for food and drink and sex. With proper use, they become good fortune. If you do not achieve the proper use of them, they become faults: being faults, what they incur is nothing but suffering. With suffering the spirit is agitated and alarmed and the soul is turned upside down.

Little do people realize that before anger and joy arise, they are the same as the buddhas and ancestral teachers. If they go wrong with anger, they become asuras. If they go wrong with ignorance, they become animals. If they go wrong with greed, they become hungry ghosts. If they go wrong with evil, they become hell-beings. Devas and humans are so by means of the ten virtues and the five precepts. These are the so-called 'six paths.'

Nevertheless, a deva who does not awaken can become a human. A human who does not awaken can become an animal. With such a multitude of faults, it would be impossible for them to return to their true state without using the water of emptiness to wash them away.

Moreover, there are three kinds of not awakening: confusion due to views and thoughts, confusion due to the multiplicity of sense objects, and fundamental ignorance. All with blood and breath are guilty of these three: that's why they do not attain to the Path of the sages. They do not penetrate to inner truth, they do not fuse phenomena, and they do not get the subtle wonder of the Path. If they penetrated inner truth, they would comprehend wherever they go. With fusion, no phenomena could obstruct them. With subtle wonder, they could encompass emptiness and existence without getting entangled. In this way ready-made subtle function would be complete in each and every one.

We people today have a tremendous accumulation of good and evil—the mountain of self and others is high. When things go against us, we are angered and displeased. When joy and anger are born, the substratum of luminous awareness is obscured. Once this pedestal of awareness is obscured, when we see form, we are deluded by form, and when we hear sounds, we are deluded by sounds.

Fragrant and foul, sweet and bitter, rough and smooth, the shadows of likes and dislikes—these are all forms of knowledge generated from sense objects. Since the knowledge is deluded, it goes wrong; going wrong, it moves away from reality. The one round light is fragmented into the six consciousnesses. Once it becomes discriminating consciousness, it judges the body to be the self. Deluded by sexual attraction, increased by desires for food and drink, the waves of sentiment flood out, washing you along into impermanence. This creates all sorts of evil manifestations in the skull's cave of false imaginations. The sky cannot cover them, the earth cannot bear them up. Tied up in the dark for eternal ages, changing physical shape, rising and sinking through myriad forms, the bitter suffering is indescribable. If people are bitten by mosquitos they squirm around and are not at peace. If they hear of this suffering and their minds remain unmoved, can they be called the most luminous of beings?

In essence, all suffering begins in not awakening. Since we do not awaken, where there is no (permanent) physical existence, we falsely cling to the existence of the body. Where there is no form, we falsely perceive the existence of mind. When we see that body and mind exist, we are not aware that the solid parts are the earth element, the liquid parts the water element, the warmth the fire element, and the motion the air element; we are aware that sensation depends on objects, that conception depends on sensation, that combination depends on conception, and that consciousness depends on combination. Thus we stubbornly cling to the perceptual phenomena of subject and object.

If there is the least transgression at the crucial juncture of death and birth, glory and disgrace, gain and loss, then the mind and spirit are in panic and confusion, the hair stands on end and the bones are chilled. This is for no other reason: the problem lies in not knowing how to return the solid parts of the body to the earth element, the liquid parts to the water element, the warmth to the fire element, and the motion to the air element; returning sensation to the objects, conception to sensation, combination to conception, and consciousness to combination. If you can effectively return them, then not awakening becomes awakening.

But tell me, at the moment of correct return, ultimately where are what we normally call body and mind? If you can penetrate through to this, you can transform the myriad faults into blessings and change disharmony into harmony. Then the body fills all of space without afflictions, and knowledge encompasses the myriad things without effect.

This method of contemplation uses emptiness as the road, as the first step on a thousand mile journey. Emptiness is not enlightenment. Enlightenment is our original home. But say, when the prodigal son returns home, whose family tune does he sing? Ah! You don't need someone else's strength to trim the wick of a lamp. There's just enough light to spare to illuminate all of space.

To Yuanguang

# 28: Dreaming
## (ZBJ, pp. 368b-c)

If there is actually no self when you sleep without dreaming, who controls the breathing? If you think there is a self, where is it? Without knowing how, you dream—suddenly you don't know where you are.

You must thoroughly shut off the myriad entangling causes —One moment, ten thousand years, ten thousand years, one moment. Find out where you are: only then can you discuss this matter properly.

If you come when your enthusiasm is high and leave when your enthusiasm runs out, and want to judge this matter with your thinking mind, though you may understand a little, all in all it is like casting a net at the wind—vain exertion that catches nothing.

I am mindful that you have come from afar. Soon your desire for us to meet will be fulfilled. Thus I would not dare ignore your good intentions: when things settle down I will question you in person.

You must be mindful that old age and sickness do not give us a fixed amount of time: time should not be frivolously wasted. When you gain success and fame, it is no different from wearing a garland of flowers in a dream. When you lose success and fame, it is no different than the flowers which you wear in the dream being blown down by the wind. Moved by the vanishing of the flowers, you awaken. Upon awakening, you think back on wearing the garland of flowers in the dream. The flowers in the dream vanish: when you awaken, who was wearing them? What vanished? Who is it who wakes up and knows of the flowers and the vanishing?

Thus you come to investigate this: before the self is there, where does the self suddenly come from? Once the self is there, it cannot turn things around, but in the end is turned around by them. Ultimately, where is the root of this sickness? If you can find out the root of the sickness, then everything is all right: wearing flowers, flowers vanishing, vain thoughts with eyes open, dreaming with eyes closed, not dreaming with eyes closed. It's all right whether you meet me or not, whether you praise me or slander me. If you cannot search out the root of the sickness, you are not qualified to be a Confucian, a Taoist, or a Buddhist.

These are true words. If the black karma[1] covers you thickly, you will not be able to believe fully. If the black karma is light, seeing or hearing these words, who would not be deeply affected?

To Ma Xinfu

## NOTES

1. Black Karma: "Black karma is the result of/reward for bad deeds: in hells and in other places where they receive suffering, sentient

beings are extremely oppressed by great pain and affliction. Hence it is called 'black.'" *Da Zhi Du Lun* 94, quoted in ZG, p. 333.

## 29:  A Swindle
### (ZBJ, pp. 369d-370a)

Men do not know how to make themselves important and make themselves great. Thus there are no lengths (of evil) they won't go to. Since they do not make themselves important, things become important and their own state of being becomes unimportant. Since they do not make themselves great, things become great and their own selves become minor. Thus they lose their importance and greatness and accept instead the trivial and the minor without refusing them. All inherently possess the full measure of this importance and this greatness, no matter whether old or young, worthy or foolish. It is just that they are swindled and led astray by insignificant reputation and petty profit, superficial glory and insubstantial social status. The fundamental light of each and every person shines through past, present, and future.

To Ma Zishan

## 30:  Back to Immediate Awareness
### (ZBJ, pp. 370a-b)

The mind light is originally profoundly clear. Making things subtly wondrous, it has no entanglements.

Arbitrarily producing knowledge and views, people lose that pure illumination. Thus the eye consciousness sticks to form, the ear consciousness sticks to sound, the nose consciousness sticks to smell, the tongue consciousness sticks to flavor, the body consciousness sticks to touch, and the conceptual mind's consciousnes sticks to phenomena. They run after objects and flow out, forever forgetting to return.

Little do they know that the first five consciousnesses[1] are a single awareness; only the sixth sets knowledge blazing up. If the sixth does not flare up, then what fault is there in that awareness (for the first five)? Thus it is said: "First we dwell in perfect immediate awareness,[2] before the floating dusts arise. Later we fall onto the ground of the conceptual faculty's 'clear understanding' and external shapes form beneath the surface. Thus perfect awareness becomes defective."

Only if you can awaken to this submerged arising of forms, and in the arena of adverse and favorable circumstances and right and wrong and glory and disgrace, thoroughly extend yourself to contemplate lucidly all gain and loss as clouds touching rock, as wind moving across the treetops, only then can you live up to being a man, and be a model of leaving home. If you spurn this responsibility, dying is better than living. When you complete the embodiment of it, then the defective one becomes perfect, and even shitting and pissing are Buddhist acts, not just burning incense.

To Zen man Quan

## NOTES

1. The first five consciousnesses and the sixth consciousness: The first five consciousnesses are associated with seeing, hearing, taste, smell, and touch. The sixth consciousness is the conceptual faculty; the seventh is *manas*, which accounts for value judgment and intentionality and motivation. The eighth consciousness is the storehouse consciousness, the *ālaya*, which contains the seeds of all phenomena and all experiences. See ZJL, pp. 773, 831-32. "The five sense faculties and the eighth consciousness are all linked to immediate awareness: they get the inherent nature of all phenomena, without bringing along names and categories, and without duality. . . . The sixth and seventh consciousnesses fall into comparative awareness: they entail assessment and arbitrary discrimination." ZJL, p. 723.

2. Immediate Awareness: see #4 note 1.

## 31:   Life Without Entanglements
### (ZBJ, p. 370c)

Ordinary people know to value life, but they do not know the means by which to nurture life.  Therefore, they are entangled by life.

Perfected people know that the way to nurture life is based on birthlessness.  Thus they can look on birth as unborn, and be born without birth, born without material entanglements.

Alas!  The eyes are entangled by form, the ears are entangled by sound, and so on.  The mind is entangled by the seven sentiments (joy, anger, sadness, fear, love, hate, and craving) and the five desires (for sights, sounds, odors, tastes, and contact).  Still, people say: "My whole life I have been happy and without entanglements."  Little do they realize that the one "without entanglements" has been entangled for a long time already.  In sum, this is because the desires of ordinary people are strong, and their spirits befuddled—they persist in their faults, unaware of them.  The ordinary person is like a drunkard lying in a mud puddle.  Someone arouses him and says, "This mud puddle is no place to be lying down in."  The drunkard glares angrily and says, "I have never drunk alcohol—why do you slander me?"

These days the whole world suffers from the drunkard's illness.  How can I find one who isn't drunk to talk with?

## 32:   Urgency
### (ZBJ, p. 374c)

Once there was a monk who had spent his whole life working on the monastery's permanent endowment, and had put off practicing.  One day he was arrested by a demon emissary.  The monk said: "Please report to Yama that I plead for seven days to practice, after which I will die without resentment."  The demon emissary said: "If your request is granted, I will return after seven days.  Otherwise I will return immediately."  The monk was allowed to practice for seven days.  Later the demon emissary came back to carry out the previous agreement, but the monk could not be found.

Ah! Birth and death is indeed a great matter! This monk advanced energetically for seven days, and even one as severe as Yama could not do anything about him. How much less could the alternation of polarities in the process of natural creation mold him!

You people have generated the aspiration to recite a verse. If your intent to advance energetically is not as decisive as this monk's, then even if you recite the verse for seven hundred days, it will do no good.

## 33: The Universal Light
### (ZBJ, p. 375a)

In our language 'Vairocana' means 'Light shining everywhere.'[1] I have always taken this to heart. Since it says that the light shines everywhere in all places, it means that everything with blood and breath is never for an instant not within this light, whether shitting or pissing, whether moving or still.

How then does it happen that when the ten evils[2] influence them, the characteristics of hell appear? So it goes through the various planes of existence, until the buddha-nature of causal conditions influences them, and the body of the Tathāgata appears. Tell me, when the marks of hell appear, ultimately where is the body of the Tathāgata? When the purple and gold of the Tathāgata's body appear, where are the marks of hell? If you can pick them out, if you can see through this, then the majestic spiritual light of mere insects does not yield a bit to the Tathāgata Vairocana's.

Now you are taking the great vow to turn the wheel of the fundamental Dharma within an atom of dust. If you can split open this atom of dust, then sense objects have no starting point. If you cannot split it open, then it will not be easy to turn the wheel of the fundamental Dharma.

## NOTES

1. Vairocana: The Universal Illuminator appears in various scriptures. In the *Hua Yan*, Vairocana dwells in the realm of the Lotus Treasury: his light shines through all worlds, and through his pores he exudes countless nirmāṇakāya buddhas to teach in all worlds. In the *Brahmajāla Sūtra* Vairocana from his Lotus world sends out a thousand Śākyamuni Buddhas to the thousand petal-worlds surrounding his abode; each petal-world contains millions of worlds and millions of buddhas teaching in them. See ZG, p. 1055.

2. The ten evils: three of the body (murder, robbery, and sexual excess), four of the mouth (false words, dirty talk, coarse words, duplicitous words sowing dissension), and three of the mind (greed, lust, and anger). ZG, p. 479.

# 34: Recovering Lost Mind
### (ZBJ, pp. 376d-377a)

If you are able to find urgency in 'recovering lost mind,'[1] but you do not know where mind is, can mind actually be recovered? If you cannot discover where mind is, then mind can never be known.

If you want to recover mind without first knowing your mind, I wonder if in what you are "recovering" there is actually a mind that can be recovered or not. Thus we realize that there is no way in the world to be able to recover mind without first knowing where it is. If you let a chicken or a dog get away and you wanted to recover them, if you did not know where they were, you could never recover them no matter how many times you called to them.

In general, if the habit of using the name but confusing the meaning is not smashed, then the road of accurately mastering the meaning and entering into its spirit is blocked.

Moreover, mind cannot be sought in terms of existence and non-existence. How can it be traced in terms of internal and external? With this physical body that appears before us, if the head is pricked the head is aware of it, if the foot is pricked the foot is aware of it, and so on over the whole surface of the body. If the eighty-four thousand pores of the body were all at once pierced by eighty-four thousand needles, they would all at once be aware of it. But if they were even the thickness of paper away, thousands of pricks would not be felt.

Is this awareness actually our mind? This mind is only aware of the immediate physical environment: it knows nothing of what is beyond it. If this is mind, the sense is clear that apart from the physical body there is no awareness. When this body decays, does this awareness actually decay along with it or not?

As for the notion that it does decay along with it: The body has form and thus is perishable and decays. But mind is fundamentally formless, so existence and non-existence cannot exhaust it. How could it decay along with the body? Since it does not decay following the body upon death, how could it be that before death it is only able to encompass the immediate physical environment but know nothing of the rest? Analyzing this in principle, it will always be hard to comprehend. A man of old had a saying: "Not only is true mind not based on form, but even false mind is not necessarily based on form."

What's the reason for this? It is because if we seek mind inside or outside, it is nowhere. How could something that is nowhere inside or outside be based on form? Thus we know that the most important point in recovering lost mind is first to awaken and understand that false mind has no essential being. Then what has drawn us on and inveigled us cannot by itself create a relativity there (between us and it).

Ah! Things and self have nothing to go back to. Who lost mind? Who will recover it? Recovery and loss, loss and recovery —if you can penetrate through this, it's like finding the nose-rope when herding an ox. You can lead it to the eastern field and you can lead it to the southern field. After leading it around for a long time it becomes pure, and then it can be gathered in or let go, gathered in and gathered in, let go and let go.

Given that you have the will for learning, it would be misleading to devote your abilities to something else and not to this (study of Mind). If you have clearly understood this Mind, then you can be a Confucian, a Buddhist, or a Taoist. If you do not understand this, then you are not a real Confucian or a real Taoist or a real Buddhist. You should work on it!

To Mr. Mao and Mr. Wu

NOTES

1. Lost mind: The phrase comes from *Mencius* 6 A 11: "Benevolence (*ren*) is the mind of man; righteousness (*yi*) is the road for man. To abandon this road and not follow it, to lose this mind and not know how to seek it—how lamentable! If people have a chicken or dog that gets lost, they know to look for it. But they have a mind that is lost, and they do not know to look for it. The Path of Learning is none other than seeking lost mind."

## 35: A Talk to the Assembly on New Year's Eve
### (ZBJ, pp. 380b-381a)

Everyone, today is the last day of the year.

> In the color of the plum blossoms
> A new year is added
> In the sound of firecrackers
> The old year wanes

I ask each of you to still the mind linked to objects and truly hear these lines spoken by Ciyun.[1]

In general people do not consider birth and death urgent. They are busied, pressed on, interrupted, scattered, and blocked by concerns over wealth and rank.

Among humans, the pinnacle of wealth and rank is the monarch. Among the gods, it is the maheśvara, the supreme ruler. But when their good fortune runs out and the signs of decline appear, their retinue departs and their majesty dwindles. When the demon of death appears before them, of course they want to act the master forcibly, but after enjoying their fool's paradise for so long, what can they do about unfeeling impermanence, which directly summons them to depart? When they reach this point in time, they are no different from the common people.

Ciyun saw right before his eyes fellows who gather together to sharpen their teeth chattering about worldly advantage. One and all they wholly focus their minds and wills on success and fame and wealth and rank as the ultimate standards. Longing and dreaming of these, they will not stop until their desires are fulfilled. In the last analysis, human monarchs and the rulers of the gods are just models of this sort. How much they suffer as they exhaust their spirits pursuing the waves, wasting a whole lifetime.

There is another sort whom wealth and rank cannot trap. What they cherish is a sense of ease and release so that they can mold their feelings into something lofty and noble. Little do they realize (the limitations of this). Among gods and humans, none is more free and at ease than the spirit immortals: riding the wind back and forth, they travel ten thousand miles in the blink of an eye; whatever their minds turn toward, everything is as they wish. But one day the reward (of this life) fades away, and they sink down into birth and death. Among all their former spiritual powers and magical transformations, from all their farflung freedoms, there is not one thing to rely on. According to their deeds, they are subject to suffering, just like the pigs and dogs. Thus they repay the debts of their deeds.

Everyone, since ancient times even those with wealth and rank and those with freedom and ease have all ended up like this when they meet the last day of their lives. Concerning those who are poor and lowly and those who are harried and pressed, what more needs to be said? This is the pattern of suffering and joy within the triple world.

What's more, all of you probably do not know that there is also suffering and joy outside the triple world. Does everyone believe this or not? If you say you do not, how dare you not believe Buddha's true words?

Śrāvakas cut off the confusion of perceptions and thoughts completely. They are forever free of the impure physical body. With the six pervasive powers[2] they act freely without contrivance: by means of them they directly cross any barriers. They can change their bodies and physical make-up as they wish. Is this not blissful joy?

Yet śrāvakas still have the confusion of the multiplicity of sense objects and fundamental ignorance too. It is hard for them to avoid the changes of birth and death. Since they have not yet completely penetrated through to buddha-nature, they become drunk on the cloudy wine of nirvāṇa, and in contact with phenomena are blocked. They are like dried out sticks, like dead men. Is this not suffering?

So this is suffering and joy outside the triple world. It obstructs buddha-nature so that one does not get the use of the samādhi of true nirvāṇa. How much the more blocked off from buddha-nature are those in the triple world with their smelly physical bodies, so dangerous and fragile, and their crazy upside-down conceptions knitting together their karma, who long for the snot and drool of wealth and rank.

If you are really fellows with blood under your skin, and clear vision in your eyes, when you hear of this kind of talk, your face will get hot and you will experience insight: you will seek a way to escape from this trap. Everyone of you has something that is very ordinary and very special: it's just that you yourselves do not know about it. Why is it very ordinary? Because all people inherently have it fundamentally and spontaneously ready-made. It's because it is locked up and sealed by emotional consciousness that you do not get the use of it. Why is it very special?

Without leaving this smelly impure body, right within this nest of the karma of affliction, you generate a firm mind of faith. Brave and bold, you advance energetically, paying no attention to gain and loss, slander and praise. Having achieved this will power, you meet true enlightened teachers, and with a straightforward mind tell them the intention you harbor. They will certainly not spurn your true sincerity. They are sure to point out to you methods for finding a living road. Accept their words directly: don't try to figure them out, don't pretend to be intelligent and make up bogus opinions. A newborn baby's only thought is of milk: he doesn't know whether his mother is good looking or ugly, high ranking or lowly. Fellows who study Zen must be like this. In sum, if the person is not genuine, if his heart is not pure, he will definitely not be able to do these things.

If you have actually accomplished this kind of inner quality, tie yourself to your basic meditation saying, and keep working carefully and continuously for days and months, until it appears clearly—a single unbreakable realm where the barriers of sentiment are cut off and conceptual consciousness does not operate. When you arrive at this state, when you search your heart, not a bit of hate or love can be found, much less physical death and birth.

At this juncture, gather your spiritual energy and go all out to advance directly till you reach enlightenment. If you do not retreat from your true mind, all the buddhas of the ten directions along with all the celestial powers will surely feel compassion for you and help you in mysterious ways. Suddenly you penetrate through—the great work is completely accomplished. Then you are free to kill or give life. There is nothing to prevent you from achieving wealth and high rank in order to spread the teaching widely, or showing a lofty and noble demeanor in order to inspire conventional worldly people. If you insist that wealth and rank or freedom and ease obstruct the Path, this is tying yourself down without ropes, and being too rigid.

If you actually reach this stage, without leaving the stinking bag of skin, you are a bodhisattva in the flesh. You extract the nails and pull out the pegs for living beings, transforming the ordinary into the sage. You wander freely on Vairocana's head, propagating the teaching amidst current conditions, repudiating the dishonesty of the "heroes" who study Zen in a dead way, striking down with blows and shouts the habit energies of ignorant fellows. If you are like this, not only do you comprehend for yourself, but you also act for other people. Isn't this very special?

Tell me, all of you, what is your basic meditation saying? Zhaozhou asked Touzi: "How is it after the person who has died the Great Death returns to life?" Touzi said: "He mustn't go by night, he must arrive in daylight."[3]

If anyone can understand, let him come forward and spit it out so we can see. If no one comprehends, let each of you do what he must.

The verse says:

> A moment of ignorance
> Obscures one's own luminous awareness
> Submerged in darkness—how many thousand births?
> Distinguishing good looking and ugly
> Among the shells of stinking corpses
> In the gates of empty illusion
> Arousing love and hate
> Sunk deep in perverted paths—
>     who knows the danger?
> Drifting in the sea of sorrow
> Not knowing how to awaken.
> Don't say that this is idle tongue-flapping
> The great need is for everyone to come out
>     of the fiery pit!

## NOTES

1. Ciyun (1274-1345) eminent monk of the Yuan period.

2. The six pervasive powers: *abhijñā, shen tong.* The power to see anything anywhere, the power to hear anything anywhere, the power to know the thoughts of other minds, the power to know the former lives of self and others, the power to go anywhere, and the power to end defilement. ZG, p. 1319.

3. Zhaozhou asked Touzi: this *gong an* is thoroughly discussed as Case 41 of the *Blue Cliff Record.* Touzi (845-914) was in the

third generation after Shitou. For his biography see CDL, j. 15, and BCR, pp. 446-47.

## 36: Desire
### (ZBJ, p. 382c)

Ordinary people are consumed by desire. Only the sages are able to consume desire. When you are consumed by desire, you lose yourself in delusion and pursue things. If you can consume desire, then nothing can turn you around. Thus the saying: "If you can transform desires, you are the same as the tathāgatas."

Once ordinary people become involved in the realms of desire, all they know is the desired object, they do not know themselves. Only the sages are without desire amidst desire. Thus they can make the myriad things subtly wondrous without being entangled by them.

## 37: Refining Oblivion and Scattering
### (ZBJ, pp. 384a-b)

In refining oblivion and scattering, if we trace back the starting point, it has been passed down and received in turn by all the buddhas of past, present, and future.

It depends on how it is used. If you truly use it well, you disperse oblivion and scattering in an instant and uphold cessation and contemplation amidst the great stillness. You drop mountains and rivers into the ground of non-existence and remove body and mind to the home of non-attainment. You cut off the sharp blades of the ties of desires and rely on the true mandate of the body of luminous awareness. The result is seen in your courage as your mind roams before creation. The light of the inherent spiritual jewel shines in your hand. There has never been anything else as precious: what can match its value? Right within the ordinary body you experience the buddha body. Based on the conventional truth, you arrive at the real truth. The achievement is lofty, spanning the sky: the merit is immeasurable. For the person who truly practices in this way, if oblivion and scattering are purified for one moment, then he is a buddha for one moment.

Alas! In the vast and boundless sea of suffering, all those with blood and breath have inside them luminous awareness, but they appear and disappear unaccountably. If a person can begin at the starting point and purify oblivion and scattering for a breath or a moment, and so become a buddha for a breath or a moment, when viewed with the enlightened eye, the accomplishment is truly inconceivable. How much the more so if you can purify oblivion and scattering for many hours and days!

In sum, what's important for people is to turn around and reflect back on themselves. If you can actually reflect back, has your own oblivion and scattering ever stopped for an instant in your whole life? Thus it is said: "If a person sits quietly for an instant, it is better than building countless jeweled stūpas." Ultimately even jeweled stūpas turn to dust, but in a moment of still mind, you achieve true enlightenment. Even if sometimes you do not use it well, you still will not lose the field of merit of humans and devas.

Therefore monks and laypeople who are virtuous and able, if they are good talkers, should travel and propagate the Dharma; if they have strength, they should protect and uphold and support the Dharma in every way. Wherever there is a center of Buddhist teaching, they should help it along with an impartial mind.

## 38: Reciting the Buddha-Name
### (ZBJ, pp. 384c-d)

A monk called on Zibo from Haizhou (in Jiangsu). Zibo asked him: "Why did you leave home?" He said: "To seek to escape suffering." Zibo asked: "What method do you use to seek to escape suffering?" The monk said: "My character is dull: I just recite the buddha-name." Zibo said: "When you recite the buddha-name, are there interruptions or not?" The monk said: "When I close my eyes and sleep it's forgotten." Zibo gave a mighty shout and said:

If you recite the buddha-name like this, forgetting as soon as you close your eyes, then it won't do any good to recite for ten thousand years. From now on you must recite the buddha-name without interruption when sleeping and dreaming: only then will you be qualified to escape suffering. If you cannot recite the buddha-name while sleeping and dreaming, if you forget it, then as soon as you open your eyes, the crying starts again.

Go before Buddha and knock your head on the ground until the blood flows. Recite the buddha-name perhaps a thousand or ten thousand times, not stopping until you have used your whole strength. If you do this twenty or thirty times, it will naturally come to be that remembrance of buddha is uninterrupted amidst the great dark sleep.

Now people in the world who recite the buddha-name may do so for twenty or thirty years; sometimes they recite the buddha-name their whole lives. But when they reach the time when they are facing death, after all it's no use. This is because in sleep and dreams before this birth they had no remembrance.

Human life is like being awake. Death is like dreaming. Thus people who have remembrance of buddha in dreams are naturally unperturbed when facing death.

## 39: Reciting the Buddha-Name Truly
### (ZBJ, pp. 384d-385a)

The method of reciting the buddha-name is the simplest and most convenient. But many of the people who recite the buddha-name these days are totally lacking in determination. Therefore of the hundreds and thousands of people who recite the buddha-name, not one or two are successful.

All the bodhisattvas, devas and human beings who are born

in the Western Paradise base themselves on this one phrase 'Amida Buddha' to cross the sea of suffering.

What is the key test of whether their minds are genuine or not as they recite the buddha-name? We get the proof when they are happy or annoyed: whether their minds are true or false can be judged clearly. Generally people who recite the buddha-name with a mind that is genuine are sure to keep reciting it without interruption while they are happy or annoyed. Because of this, neither happiness nor annoyance can move them. Since neither vexation nor joy can move them, naturally they are not alarmed at scenes of death and birth. These days people recite the buddha-name, but when the least joy or anger arises, Amida Buddha is tossed to the back of their minds. How can they get the spiritual effect of reciting the buddha-name?

If you recite the buddha-name as I recommend, you will be able not to ignore this phrase 'Amida Buddha' at junctures of hate and love. In your present daily activities you will get the use of it and when you are facing the end you will be reborn in the Western Paradise. If it is not so, my tongue is sure to rot. If you do not practice according to my method, then reciting the buddha-name will have no spiritual effect—the fault lies with you, it has no connection to me.

## 40: Reciting Dhāraṇī[1]
### (ZBJ, pp. 385a-b)

People's conscious minds have been mixed up with sensory affliction for a long time, and don't know how to return to the basis. If you want to merge with enlightened nature right amidst sensory afflictions, you should avail yourself of the practice of reciting dhāraṇīs. There is more than one method for doing this, but how could any be better than the esoteric basis of the tathāgatas, the dhāraṇī of total command?

What's the reason? According to whether people's faculties were sharp or dull, the buddhas left behind teachings that vary in relative depth and are not the ultimate teaching. It's only with reciting these dhāraṇī that it doesn't matter whether you are stupid or smart: everyone achieves the supreme most profound rarity. This is because the esoteric basis is inconceivable.

If people open to enlightenment contemplate with a faithful mind the words of the dhāraṇī they recite, until each and every word and phrase is completely clear in their eyes, and their minds and ears together embrace the dhāraṇī without admixture or confusion, not forgetting it even in sleep and dreams—one time upholding the dhāraṇī like this is better than hundreds of thousands of (mixed mind) repetitions. It can wipe out the eighty-four thousand afflictions of sensory experience and engender the eighty-four thousand fruits of the Path. The merit this possesses is most rare and inconceivable.

Since this dhāraṇī is the fundamental vow of merit spoken by the Refulgent King Tathāgata,[2] when you are about to recite the dhāraṇī, you must pay homage nine times to the Refulgent King Tathāgata, join your palms and kneel. Recite it one hundred eight times a day. Reciting until the energy is unified, gathering in the energy, you can tether your thoughts.

Thus the sūtra says: "Let the recitation be like an awl." This means it must enter the commanding mind so that the recitation is never interrupted. Except when conversing with people, you should uphold the dhāraṇī twenty-four hours a day. You should recite it when first waking up and recite it before going to sleep. You should maintain it when you are walking, standing, sitting, and lying down. You should recite it when eating and drinking and when shitting and pissing. Thus you will uphold the recitation without a break. Generally you must maintain it silently with mouth closed, letting the sound be completely clear. This is true upholding of dhāraṇī. You will find peaceful bliss, merit, wisdom, and added power. The rarities you seek will be gained as vowed.

When you recite the dhāraṇī, have both hands clasped in diamond fists, upper and lower teeth touching, the tongue touching the very center of the roof of the mouth, the eyes constantly watching over the nose. Based on the nose (breathing), contemplate the mind. From the mind, contemplate the navel. When the pure energy of the whole body silently joins with the dhāraṇī, it subtly meshes with the Dharma of effortless contemplation. This is the bridge for entering the true nature of mind.

I hope that those who read and hear of this will joyfully accept and uphold it, uphold it firmly throughout your lives with a mind of faith that does not turn away. Those who carefully circulate this are true children of Buddha.

## NOTES

1. Dhāraṇī: Reciting dhāraṇī is a form of remembrance practice analogous to invoking the buddha-name (*nian fo*). Scriptures like the *Prajñāpāramitā* and the *Lotus* have sections on dhāraṇī, and dhāraṇī play a seminal role in esoteric Buddhism: they are considered the esoteric basis for the secret treasury of the Tathāgatas' powers. SY, p. 1251; ZG, p. 831.

"'Dhāraṇī' in Chinese means 'able to maintain' and 'able to ward off.' They are 'able to maintain' in that, having brought together all kinds of good dharmas, they can maintain them so that they are not scattered or lost. . . . They are 'able to ward off' in that if mental propensities to evil are born, they can ward them off so that they are not born. If one is about to do evil, they can hold one so that one does not do evil. This is called 'dhāraṇī.'" *Da Zhi Du Lun* 5, quoted ZG, p. 831. Given the interpenetration of noumenon and phenomena, and of phenomena with each other, any specific dhāraṇī can be a conductor to all dhāraṇīs, and to infinity.

2. The Refulgent King Tathāgata: emitting light from every pore, he sits in maṇḍalas. See Mochizuki, pp. 1847-48. There is a short scripture called *The Sūtra of the Dhāraṇī of the Refulgent King Tathāgata for Banishing All Disasters* (T 964).

# 41:   On Leaving Home
## (ZBJ, pp. 385c-d)

Monks beg for food.  Basically this is in order to keep entanglements at a distance.  If entanglements are not kept at a distance, there will be a lot of trouble: in that case, the initial aspiration for enlightenment cannot but be disturbed. This was the deep concern of our Buddha.

Yet in later generations those called monks consider begging for food shameful.  Isn't this because they haven't thought the matter through at all?  Those whom the world calls 'the mighty' just value flattery.  Thus the types who wag their tails and beg for sympathy, who understand well how to play up to them, always get the title 'director of affairs' (at the places such donors patronize).  From this point of view, the monks playing false is not only the fault of those who have left home: those at home also assist in it.

These days our own dynasty chooses officers solely in terms of achievement in the examination system.  The system of examining monks in the sūtras has fallen out of practice.  As for examination studies, basically they are useless things, used in order to tie down human sentiments, so they can be worn away over the years and months.  Choosing talented men (for government service) by this means and putting them in charge of the Tao, the moral orientation of the society, is like putting out a fire with oil—the flames only increase.  When monks are not examined in the sūtras for ordination, they don't even know the Buddha's words, so how could they know the Buddha's mind?  To be a monk without knowing the Buddha's mind— how is such a 'monk' any different from a common person? Why shave the head and wear black? (Lacuna of 20 graphs) It's not demon kings and outsiders that can destroy Buddhism— the ones who destroy it are the monks who are no different from common people.

# 42:  Ten Vows of the Universally Good One
### (ZBJ, p. 386a)

The bodhisattva Samantabhadra[1] has ten vows: each vow is of special excellence, majestic and mighty. If you attain to one vow, you will achieve enlightenment without a doubt: how much the more so if you attain to them all!

The first is to pay reverent homage to all the buddhas, so you attain excellence in the deeds of the body.

The second is to praise the tathāgatas, so you attain excellence in the deeds of the mouth.

The third is to work on a wide scale to support and nurture living beings, so you attain excellence in deeds of merit.

The fourth is to repent karmic obstructions, so that you attain purity in the three kinds of deeds (of body, mouth, and mind).

The fifth is the accomplished virtue of rejoicing in the good deeds of others, so that habits of jealousy are abruptly emptied.

The sixth is to invite the turning of the Wheel of the Dharma, so that the light of wisdom is round and full.

The seventh is to invite the buddhas to dwell in the world, so that the special excellence of the linked benefit to self and others is attained.

The eighth is always to follow the Buddha and learn, so that the life of wisdom lives forever.

The ninth is always to adapt to sentient beings, so that enemies and intimates are treated equally.

The tenth is to transfer all accomplished merit to all beings, so that barriers at the level of phenomena and of inner truth dissolve.

In the midst of your daily activities, as you encounter circumstances adverse and favorable, earnestly call out these ten vows: after long days and months you will spontaneously transform hate into love and love into hate. Through hate and love, love and hate, likes and dislikes have no constancy. But the king of vows is unmoved—he proceeds directly to wondrous enlightenment.  What difficulties or dangers are there?

## NOTES

1. Samantabhadra: bodhisattva representing universal enlightened action.  In the climactic 'Entry into the Realm of Reality' section of the *Hua Yan* are the ten vows of Samantabhadra as related here by Zibo.  In order to see Samantabhadra, the pilgrim Sudhana develops "a great mind vast as space, an unhindered mind relinquishing all worlds and free from attachments."  See T. Cleary, *Entry into the Inconceivable*, p. 9.

# 43: Four Accomplishments of the Enlightened Teachers
### (ZBJ, pp. 386c-387a)

If one cherishes people for great reasons, one's concerns are far-reaching.  If one cherishes people for petty reasons, one's concerns are shallow.  The far-reaching is hard to glimpse.  The shallow is easy to see.  Thus, one who considers it advantageous to be a tyrant does not want to be a true king.  One who considers being a king advantageous does not want to be a buddha.

The Path of the Buddhas is vast and far-reaching.  They make a single vow, establish a single practice, traversing countless eons.  If they do not succeed in one lifetime, they are born hundreds and thousands of times.  If they do not succeed in hundreds and thousands of lifetimes, they are sure to keep on being born ad infinitum.

If we have the will for the Path of the Buddhas, we view floating glory among humans and devas as less than a feather in the great void.

These days there are people who see the shallow but do not see the far-reaching, who hold to the petty and slander the great.  While teaching at Tanzhe,[1] I heard such people and pitied them, fearing that they would cut off the Buddha's life of wisdom, and incur punishment for their crime.  I borrowed metaphors from worldly teachings in order to lead them from the shallow into the deep, and make them realize that approaching success by fraud and force is not as good as opening up enlightened perception.

Enlightened perception cannot be gained by clever wisdom, nor can it be sought by means of austerities. What is important is developmental influences. But there are myriad different kinds of developmental influences. If you develop under the influence of the five transgressions and ten evils, it leads to the perceptions of hell-beings. If you develop under the influence of stinginess, it leads to the perceptions of hungry ghosts. If you develop under the influence of stupidity and ignorance, it leads to the perceptions of animals. If you develop under the influence of the five precepts and the ten virtues, it leads to the perceptions of humans and devas. If you develop under the influence of the four truths of birth and extinction, it leads to the perceptions of śrāvakas. If you develop under the influence of the twelve causal links, it leads to the perceptions or pratyekas. If you develop under the influence of the infinite four truths, it leads to the perceptions of bodhisattvas of the Particular Teaching. Only if you develop under the influence of the four truths without doing can this be called the perceptions of a buddha.[3]

Alas! In the world at the end of the Semblance Period, the wind of the End of the Dharma is high. The clouds of demons and outsiders gather in profusion. Great teachers—dragons and elephants—are rarely encountered. Not only is it difficult to foster the seeds of enlightenment, even for the seeds of being humans and devas, causal conditions are often wrong and seldom right. So much the worse for enlightened perception!

Thus I make temporary use of the water fast as the flag and drum, and use austerities as a means to influence people, to arouse their energies and strengthen their minds. I use the prajñā of written words on an intimate level to influence their understanding of causation and open the way for the development of the correct basis. I hope that those who practice along with me will open up to the reality aspect right within their unknowing "knowledge" in their daily activities as sentient beings. Since root capacities are not equal in sharpness and dullness, it is hard to accomplish this vow. While the vow is not yet accomplished, the results are not obvious. Thus there are bound to be many doubts and little certain belief. Those who doubt will slander and incur the karmic rewards of slander.

Someone said to Zibo: "You should go along a little with people's sentiments to attract people of ordinary mentalities. Wouldn't it be good to make the doubter believe and the believers develop understanding?"

Zibo gave a great relaxed laugh and said: Slander is not born alone, it is surely relative to praise. Doubt has no basis without belief. Now you want me to remold slander into praise and guide doubt into belief. This is like thinking the bent finger is bad and so getting rid of the extended finger.

Little do you realize that to be a highly respected person is easy, but to be a great person is hard. The so-called highly respected person does no more than maintain a bit of disciplined practice in a narrow-minded inflexible way. The great person just vows to benefit the whole world, and its future generations. Even if he meets with the bad name of the most notorious villains, he does not refuse the task. How can petty slanders and doubts touch him?

Generally, what ordinary people cling to is sentiment. What the perfected people carry out is wisdom. Sentiments are like solid ice, blocked at many points. Wisdom is like pure water, square or round according to the vessel.

Thus our great enlightened sage Buddha had four siddhas, four accomplishments.[4] He established the teaching according to circumstances, not bound by any constant measure. He was like a great general employing troops: he makes them act according to his orders, not necessarily understand them. If they thought they understood, sentiments would be born, and opinions of relative advantage along with them: how could they defeat the enemy?

As for the four siddhas: One is called 'worldly accomplishment,' meaning that there are limits that should not be transgressed. One is called 'the accomplishment of curing,' meaning that they see the illness and prescribe the medicine accordingly. One is called "the accomplishment of acting for people,' meaning that they follow what's best for the individual potential and situation. One is called 'supreme accomplishment,' meaning to open up correct perception. The first three siddhas are close to the samādhi of following sentiments; the last one is close to the samādhi of following wisdom.[5]

If they do not know the starting point of these four siddhas when they transmit the Dharma and propagate the Path, those who would act as the emissaries of the Tathāgata will have no leading principle inside and no guidelines on the outside. Given the least contact with the winds of situations, their standpoint is unsettled.

Again: The samādhi of following sentiments may be easy to see, but the samādhi of following wisdom is hard to glimpse. It's only to be expected that doubts and slanders will arise about the one that's hard to glimpse. You insist that I dissolve these doubts and stop these slanders. But I am not a kid: how could I act like a kid and do something that's meaningless?

At this the one who had spoken to Zibo was annoyed and left.

## NOTES

1. Tanzhe: a temple near Mt. Fang just south of the Yongding River about twenty-five miles west of Beijing.

2. Benevolence and righteousness: *ren* and *yi*, which are among the cardinal virtues of Confucianism. See #34, note 1: quote from Mencius.

3. The Four Truths: In the Tiantai analysis, each of the four levels of the Teaching has a corresponding appreciation of the Four Noble Truths. For the Storehouse Teaching, it is the four truths of birth and extinction, because they consider suffering, the arising of suffering, and the path out of suffering to have real birth and demise based on causation, and they consider the extinction of suffering as

real extinction. For the Comprehensive Teaching, it is the four truths without birth, because they view everything as an illusion, so that phenomena are empty in themselves, without birth or demise. For the Particular Teaching, it is the infinite four truths, because the forms of suffering and of the path out of it are infinite and particularized—this is the bodhisattva view. For the Round Teaching, it is the four truths without doing, because in total fusion affliction and enlightenment, nirvāna and saṃsāra, are one. SY, p. 560.

4. Four siddhas: 'accomplished powers.' This set is in the *Da Zhi Du Lun* 1, SY, p. 551.

5. Samādhi of following sentiments, samādhi of following wisdom: According to Mochizuki, p. 2868, propounded by Zhiyi in *Maha Zhi Guan* (T 497) and *Fa Hua Jing Xuan Yi* (T 1716) on the basis of Buddha's remark in the Nirvāṇa Sūtra that in preaching he had sometimes followed along with the mentalities of others, and sometimes his own, and sometimes both.

# 44: The Perfection of Meditation
## (ZBJ, pp. 387b-388b)

The practice of the perfection of meditation, dhyāna-pāramitā, has ten meanings in all. First, the great meaning. Second, interpreting the name. Third, the gate of illumination. Fourth, understanding the explanations. Fifth, the mind to choose among dharmas. Sixth, distinguishing skillful means. Seventh, explaining cultivation and realization. Eighth, manifesting the results. Ninth, from meditation, creating verbal techniques. Tenth, joining together the routes returning (to the source).

Since practitioners of beginners' mind develop their aspirations for enlightenment differently, today we will have a discussion on the great meaning, picking out errors and clarifying what's correct. We pick out errors because practitioners have different mentalities[1] in their practice of meditation, and many fall into distortions and errors.

One type aspires to practice meditation for the sake of

profit and being supported. Most of these are developing hellish mentalities. A second type aspires to practice meditation for reputation and acclaim. Most of these are developing the minds of hungry ghosts. A third type aspires to practice meditation for the sake of their families. Most of these are developing the minds of animals. A fourth type aspires to practice meditation out of jealousy, to surpass others. Most of these develop the mentalities of asuras. A fifth type aspires to practice meditation because they fear the painful rewards of evil paths, and wish to stop all evil doings. Most of these develop the mentality of humans. A sixth type aspires to practice meditation for the sake of good states of mind, for peace and bliss. Most of these are developing the mentality of the six heavens of desire. A seventh type aspires to practice meditation in order to get power and dominion. Most of these develop the deluded, demonic māra mentality. An eighth type aspires to practice meditation in order to obtain mental acuity and quickness. Most of these are developing the mentalities of the outside paths. A ninth type aspires to practice meditation in order to be born in heaven. Most of these develop the mentalities of the realm of form (beyond desire) and the formless realm. A tenth type aspires to practice meditation in order to cross over the sufferings of old age, sickness and death, and quickly attain nirvāṇa. These develop the mentality of the Two Vehicles.

These ten types of practitioners differ in relative degrees of good and bad, of bondage and liberation, but all of them lack the correct contemplation of great compassion. Since they develop their minds wrongly, none of them are the Buddha's seed. Thus I pick out their errors.

For practitioners who are correctly illuminated bodhi-sattvas, the great meaning of the perfection of meditation is twofold. But for now let's not discuss it: I fear that if ordinary people heard, they would be afraid; being afraid, they would become alarmed, become suspicious and distrustful, and give out with slander. For slander, they would incur suffering; suffering would produce rancor. When rancor is deep it forms karmic bonds. Karmic bonds make liberation impossible.

Since they cannot be freed, they will oppose the Dharma as enemies till the end. Thus, for now, let us put this aside.

Ah! Developing the mind to practice meditation is by no means easy. With your initial aspiration for enlightenment, you must meet a clear-eyed enlightened teacher to set straight the causal ground for you. Otherwise, even if you fast like Bo Yi and Shu Ji,[2] even if you endure pain like Mo Di, even if you work hard for ten thousand ages, you will be blocked off from the Buddha's enlightenment by both existence and non-existence. Thus the saying: "If discipline is slow, but the teaching vehicle is fast, it's not slow. If the discipline is fast, but the teaching vehicle is slow, it's really slow."

During our water fast, we have engaged in the practice of wisdom and the practice of action in order to temper and control sentiments and habit patterns. We have gone through all sorts of expedient means, relying on them and using them in turn. Overall, the practice of wisdom has been the principal means, aided by the practice of action. Before a single seven day period was up, we felt our bodies and minds lighten and become sharp. Things we had heard in the scriptures that caused us doubts or difficulties that we could not explain, spontaneously emptied out and became free from sticking points. All sentiments and habit patterns too emptied out and fell away.

If we were to take the practice of action as primary and the practice of wisdom as an auxiliary, we would grind away for many days, but the benefit gained would not match the benefit of taking the practice of wisdom as primary and the practice of action as auxiliary. This being so, let us each feel shame that our practice of wisdom is meagre and inferior, and that there are still many obstacles for us among the elements of sensory experience to our entering cessation by means of contemplation and entering contemplation by means of cessation, that we still blunder into confusion amidst forms and appearances.

So let us inquire again into what Zhiyi, the great teacher of Tian Tai, said about the perfection of meditation in such writings as the *Great Cessation and Contemplation* and the

*Aid to Practice.*[3] These fully reveal the practice of wisdom and let us know more about levels and priorities of the practice of action. This will not only be an aid to our own progress in cultivation. For those who do water fasts in the future, it will show how those who first develop their aspiration for enlightenment must first investigate the proper basis in the causal ground, so that they will not go against what the sages were faithful to. Therefore I have patched on this account of ten kinds of distortions and errors in developing the mind for enlightenment, to serve as a guiding mirror.

Nevertheless, if we look for an account of water fasting in the Canon, we don't see a scriptural basis for it. But this method has been handed down: for a day and a night, three handfuls of sesame seeds and twenty-one dates, eaten in three portions. This is considered the set form at both Zhong Nan and Fu Niu.[4] Some take the buddha-remembrance as their meditation point, some take reciting dhāraṇī as their meditation point.

Then there are those who go on the water fast, but just follow their own ideas, dragging out the days in oblivion and scattering. They do not even hear the names 'practice of wisdom' 'practice of action'—how could they know their meanings? If you do not know the meanings of these, what will you base your contemplation on? If you don't do contemplation, how will you enter cessation? If you do not enter cessation, grasping at objects does not cease, so the mind ground is not pure. When the mind ground is not pure, affliction blazes. Ablaze with affliction, the form of self solidifies. When the self aspect solidifies, you become attached and cling to the stinking skin bag. Thus you make body and mind self-contradictory. In movement and in stillness you preserve error in myriad forms.

Words in themselves are not good or bad. If they accord with your sentiments, even if they are of no benefit to you, you are pleased and happy to hear them. If they go against your sentiments, even if they would benefit you, you get angry and don't like to hear them.

Little do you know: all who study Buddhism must first

reach the realization that afflictions and entanglements are causally linked to having a body. By not staying concerned with the body you stop affliction. You should know that repeated birth is due to holding to transformation, and not going along with transformation to seek the source. If you act like this, if you become greatly attached to the stinking skin bag, if you create protected prejudices within the mind of affliction, isn't this staying concerned with the body and holding to transformation? If you stay concerned with the body, there is no shedding afflictions and entanglements, and birth and death is hard to escape. If you hold to transformation, emotional consciousness does not dry up. If emotional consciousness does not dry up, when can you emerge from the sea of suffering and affliction?

With failings like these, the problem lies in perception being unilluminated. Perception is the practice of wisdom. Equipped with the practice of wisdom, you have an undefiled basis to rely on in the practice of action. Without the practice of wisdom, there will always be defilement. Defilement is the same as the nine kinds of distortions and errors in developing mind in the foregoing discussion picking out errors. They make it hard to rise and easy to fall. They are definitely not bridges out of suffering. They should be feared and dreaded.

Therefore, if you haven't got the know how of the practice of wisdom and the practice of action, you haven't even found out about the lesser vehicles' view of the truth, much less the views of the truth in the Beginning, Final, Sudden, and Round Teachings.[5] Thus, without a view of the truth as the basis, going on a water fast will never be a correct basis for enlightenment. Even if you fasted on water all your life, it would have nothing to do with your own personal task. Nevertheless, compared to those who indulge themselves in luxurious excess and are never willing to eat simple fare, fasting on water is indeed to be respected.

When going on water fasts in northern lands where it is very cold, ginger can be taken as wished. If there is constipation, drink honey water.

It is only the great Tathāgata who knows from experience with perfect accuracy what is to be permited and what is to be forbidden to body and mind. Thus, in the section on precepts, the vinaya, there are restraints directed at sentiments; according to the situation, they can be lifted or imposed. For example, a bhikṣu is not permitted to wear boots and fur cloaks, but in countries that are very cold, this is lifted. Those in the future who go on water fasts should make this their model.

Someone said: "Teacher, you said that you were afraid that if ordinary people heard the great meaning of practicing meditation for those who are bodhisattvas, they would not believe it, and in the end this would lead to rancor and opposition. How could such a thing happen?"

Zibo replied: Bodhidharma, our first ancestral teacher,[6] crossed mountains and sailed the seas to come to this land—he did not consider ten thousand *li* far to come. He sought nothing else but this: having awakened to his own inherent mind, he felt compassion for those who had not yet awakened. Thus he came, not shrinking from cold or heat, his sole purpose to deliver living beings. Yet crooked teachers, demons and outsiders plotted against him countless times, and even poisoned him six times. The great Zen teacher Si of Nanyue[7] experienced bodily the station of the purity of the six senses, yet he too was poisoned, dying and reviving several times. Both of them were sages, with spreading the Dharma as their purposes, and not even they could avoid (such hostility), so how could we, we whose views and thoughts are not yet cut off, whose compartmentalized distinctions still remain? If we do not shut our mouths and check our tongues, if we disguise our ignorance and peddle our folly, then this mandate 'to investigate reality-nature to the end' has been long lost!

Someone asked: "You left home because of birth and death: why do you fear death?" Zibo laughed and said: Whether one fears death or not is not a matter of strong talk. Just watch him when it's about time to get out, then you'll know.

## NOTES

1. Hell, hungry ghosts, animals, asuras, humans, heavens of desire: These are the so-called 'six paths' or planes of existence in the realm of desire. In Chan style, Zibo relates them to various states of mind. The six heavens then refer to certain sublime states in the upper reaches of the realm of desire. Above the realm of desire is the realm of pure form, reached through meditation in four levels. Then there is the formless realm, at the pinnacle of meditational accomplishment: states of infinite space, infinite consciousness, total nothingness, and neither thought nor no thought. "If you maintain the low kind of discipline, you are born among humans. If you maintain the middle kind of discipline, you are born in the six desire heavens. If you maintain the high kind of discipline, and also practice the four levels of meditation and the four empty concentrations, you are born in the pure heavens of the realm of form and the formless realm." *Da Zhi Du Lun* 13, quoted ZG, p. 1320.

2. Bo Yi and Shu Ji are the proverbial martyrs to loyalty who went into seclusion at the end of the Yin dynasty (traditionally, twelfth century B.C.E.) and starved to death rather than eat the food of the succeeding dynasty, the Zhou. ZW, p. 928.

3. *Great Cessation and Contemplation* and *Aid to Practice: Maha Zhi Guan* (T 497) and *Zhi Guan Bu Xing Hong Chuan Jue* (T 1912).

4. Zhong Nan and Fu Niu: in Shanxi and Henan respectively, these two mountains were religious centers frequented by Taoists and Buddhists.

5. Beginning, Final, Sudden, and Round Teachings: This is the division of the teachings of the Hua Yan School. In the Lesser Vehicle, they do not know that the myriad phenomena exist because of mind. Since they do not awaken to the mind source, they cling to the lesser fruits: they wipe away form and cling to emptiness. In the Beginning Teaching of the Great Vehicle, they do not wipe out form and cling to emptiness, because they know that form itself is empty. They know that all phenomena are causally born, and hence without fixed identity. Though they witness this reality, they still have moment to moment birth and destruction, so there is contrived action (to deal with it). For the Final Teaching of the Great Vehicle, they attain interfusion of phenomena and noumenon: nature and form are synthesized

and root and branch are equalized. For the Sudden Teaching, in a moment unborn, you are buddha. All things have always and of themselves been in nirvāṇa: from sentient beings to buddhas, from enlightenment to saving beings, all is like a dream. For the Round Teaching, the interpenetration of the one and the many, the centers and the satellites, reduplicating to infinity without obstruction, is fully in view. As the *Hua Yan* says: "There is no suchness outside of wisdom which is entered by wisdom and no wisdom outside suchness which can witness suchness." ZJL, pp. 571-72.

6. Bodhidharma: the First Patriarch of Chan. See BCR Case 1 and p. 225.

7. Huisi of Nanyue (515-577): the teacher of Zhiyi, founder of Tiantai. See Hurvitz, *Chi-I*, pp. 108-110.

# Bibliography

## Reference Works

Goodrich, L. C., editor. *Dictionary of Ming Biography.* New York, 1976.

Mochizuki Shinko. *Bukkyo Daijiten* [Dictionary of Buddhism]. Tokyo, 1955-1963.

SY: *Shiyong Foxue Cidian* [Practical Use Buddhist Studies Dictionary]. Taibei, 1974.

ZG: *Zengaku Daijiten* [Zen Studies Dictionary]. Tokyo, 1979.

ZW: *Zhongwen Da Cidian* [Dictionary of Literary Chinese]. Taibei, 1963.

## Buddhist Works

BCR: Cleary T. and J. C. *The Blue Cliff Record.* Boulder and London, 1977.

CDL: *Chuan Deng Lu* [Record of the Transmission of the Lamp] (published 1004). Taibei, 1956.

Cleary, J. C. *Swampland Flowers: Letters and Lectures of Zen Master Ta Hui.* New York, 1977.

Cleary, J. C. *Zen Dawn.* Boston, 1986.

Cleary, T. *Entry into the Inconceivable: an Introduction to Hua-yen Buddhism.* Honolulu, 1983.

Cleary, T. *The Flower Ornament Scripture.* Boulder and London, 1984.

Cleary, T. *The Original Face: an Anthology of Rinzai Zen.* New York, 1978.

ZZ: *Dainihon Zokuzokyo* [Great Japanese Continuation of the Canon]. Tokyo, 1905-1912.

Hanshan Deqing. *Hanshan Dashi Meng You Quan Ji* [The Complete Collection of Hanshan's Dream Wanderings]. ZZ ji 1, bian 2, tao 32, ce 3-5.

Hanshan Deqing. *Hanshan Dashi Nianpu Shu Zheng* [Autobiography of Hanshan]. Taibei, 1966.

WDHY: *Wu Deng Hui Yuan* [Five Lamps Meeting at the Source] (preface 1253). Taibei, 1970.

Yunqi Zhuhong. *Huang Ming Ming Seng Jilue* [Outline Studies on Eminent Monks of the Imperial Ming]. ZZ ji 1, bian 2B, tao 17, ce 3.

Yunqi Zhuhong. *Yunqui Fa Hui* [Dharma Collection of Yunqi]. Nanking, 1897.

ZBBJ: *Zibo Zunzhe Bie Ji* [Separate Record of Zibo]. ZZ ji 1, bian 2, tao 32, ce 1.

ZBJ: *Zibo Zunzhe Quan Ji* [Complete Works of Zibo]. ZZ ji 1, bian 2, tao 31, ce 4-5 and tao 32, ce 1.

ZJL: Yanshou. *Zong Jing Lu* [The Source Mirror] (c. 970). Shanghai, 1935.

## Books in English of Related Interest

Egerton, Clement. *The Golden Lotus.* London, 1972. [Translation of the Ming period vernacular novel *Jin Ping Mei*, about a wealthy merchant and his six wives.]

Gallager, Joseph Louis, S. J. *The China That Was: China as Discovered by the Jesuits at the Close of the Sixteenth Century.* New York, 1953. [A translation of the journal of the intrepid missionary pioneer Matteo Ricci.]

Huang, Ray. *1587: A Year of No Significance: the Ming Dynasty in Decline.* New Haven, 1981.

Idries Shah. *Learning How to Learn.* New York, 1978. [Contemporary description of mystic religion from within.]

Overmyer, Daniel. *Folk Buddhist Religion: Dissenting Sects in Late Traditional China.* Cambridge, 1976.

Tu Wei-ming. *Neo-Confucian Thought in Action: Wang Yang-ming's Youth.* Berkeley and Los Angeles, 1967.

Yu, A. C. *The Journey to the West.* Chicago, 1977. [A translation of the Ming period vernacular novel *Xi You Ji*, a satire on religion.]

Yu Chun-fang. *The Renewal of Buddhism in China: Zhuhong and the Late Ming Synthesis.* New York, 1981.